MARKETING THROUGH MEASUREMENT

F. KEAY and G. L. WENSLEY

PERGAMON PRESS
OXFORD · NEW YORK
TORONTO · SYDNEY · BRAUNSCHWEIG

Pergamon Press Ltd., Headington Hill Hall, Oxford

Pergamon Press Inc., Maxwell House, Fairview Park, Elmsford, New York 10523

Pergamon of Canada Ltd., 207 Queen's Quay West, Toronto 1

Pergamon Press (Aust.) Pty. Ltd., 19a Boundary Street, Rushcutters Bay, N.S.W. 2011, Australia

Vieweg & Sohn GmbH, Burgplatz 1, Braunschweig

First edition 1970

Library of Congress Catalog Card No. 70–124059

Printed in Great Britain by A. Wheaton & Co., Exeter

08 015764 5 (flexicover)
08 015765 3 (hard cover)

CONTENTS

EDITOR'S INTRODUCTION

TO PARAPHRASE Lord Kelvin—if you can't measure it don't do it. For far too long it has been argued by too many marketing men that Marketing is an art, not a science. What they mean is probably that the only way to take a marketing decision is "the old Greek method" of reflection. If you think long enough, inspiration will provide the answer.

Of course there are vast areas of human behaviour that are only partially understood, and this is as true with the study of that part of human behaviour which we call marketing.

This does not mean that understanding and thus measurement is not possible, it simply means we have to make greater efforts to understand.

The purpose of this book is to start us off down the right road. The road which will lead to a better understanding of the environment in which we are operating and therefore a better opportunity to measure in real terms the efforts we are making. There is still a place for hunch, but let us measure what we can and thereby reduce the element of risk in our marketing operations.

This book is written for marketing executives and experience has shown that many marketing executives are frightened by any idea of mathematics. If this book does nothing more than reduce this fear then it will have achieved its purpose.

Cookham

D. W. SMALLBONE

INTRODUCTION

EACH age of history has its own characteristics and features that symbolise those characteristics. The symbol of the 1960's is, without much doubt, the electronic computer and the principal characteristic that it symbolises is that the sixties is the age of measurement. During this era it has become increasingly apparent that it is no longer sufficient to say that situations exist. It is necessary to say how strongly they exist.

This is true in the business context and it is as true of marketing situations as it is of general business situations. Those who are called upon to make decisions in the field of marketing as of business generally are required to come to terms with this new fact of business life. Regret it they may: ignore it they dare not. This accepted, difficulty faces the manager in how to come to terms with it. The prospect of studying mathematics may daunt him and in any case it is an unnecessary step. He can always hire expertise in mathematics.

If he does, however, he faces the difficulty of trying to understand what the mathematician is saying to him and of explaining to the mathematician what he wants him to do. It is not the complete answer to say that the mathematician must learn the language of the businessman. The mathematician can be asked to do something about it but he should not be required to speak only in plain language because each specialist human activity acquires a language of its own in which its thinking is most effectively expressed and every step taken away from its natural language brings a diminution in the effectiveness of its operations.

So the gulf exists and only too often is allowed to remain without any attempt made to narrow it. The modern manager, however, is capable of learning enough of the specialist's language to comprehend him. Some do and if all would, the resultant improvement in mutual understanding would be great. If an effective dialogue can not be mounted between the manager and the technocrat, either the technocrat is ignored or the manager is in his hands.

This book is an attempt to put before the marketing decision-maker some of the concepts of measurement which he will come across in his field. It is in no way intended to provide a means of enabling the marketing manager to "do it himself" but it is hoped that a study of the book will enable the marketing manager to come to terms with his experts in measurement and analysis, to feel at ease with them and above all to know the right sort of questions to ask them.

It is by no means exhaustive of all the techniques that are coming into use but it is hoped that it covers those which are at the time of writing sufficiently proven as to be in fairly common use. An understanding of those included would enable a marketing decision-maker to widen his knowledge to include newer techniques as they became more strongly established. Further reading would be necessary if it were desired to practise the techniques in any but the simpler situations. A bibliography is included for those who might wish to pursue studies in this direction.

Many friends and colleagues have given advice and help in the preparation of this book. They are too numerous to mention by name individually, but the thanks of the authors are due to them. *Marketing through Measurement* is a better book than it would have been without their help.

Special thanks must be expressed to Mrs. Sheila Faulkner and to Mrs. June Scoones who typed the various drafts in which the script appeared and to Mrs. Sylvia Luke for drawing the diagrams. The authors, finally, are grateful to the publishers and to the Principal of Ashridge Management College for their encouragement.

CHAPTER 1

THE MARKETING PROBLEM

ALL human activity results in the creation of goods or services which, whether by conscious design or not, satisfy some need or desire. Sometimes the creator and the ultimate consumer are one and the same person as, for example, when a housewife cooks herself a meal or knits herself a jumper. Services, too, can be rendered to oneself, a fact well known to the home-decorator or to the man servicing his own car. With goods and services created by groups the case is normally different. Such groups banded together as a commercial or trade organisation are creating goods or providing services designed for the satisfaction of others although, of course, individual members of the group may be consumers also.

Group activity differs from individual activity in another respect also. Except in the case of philanthropic institutions all group activity is performed with the intention that it should make a profit. For this to happen, the worth of the goods or services to the consumer, expressed by the value of what he is prepared to give in exchange for them, must be greater than the cost of producing them. The mechanism by which this profit is produced is the activity of marketing and the marketing problem is to discover the factors which affect this mechanism and to understand as much as possible of their nature.

The mechanism functions by ensuring that the right goods are available for the right customer at the right time in the right place and at the right price. The discovery of what are the right goods for the right customer, what is the right place, the right time and what is the right price are all parts of the marketing

1

problem. There is no single set of factors exerting an influence equally on all the parts of the problem. Each part requires to be examined separately and its own individual factors identified. The chapters of this book deal in turn with these separate parts.

In marketing, as in all other areas of activity, questions of leadership arise but this book does not deal with leadership matters. The leadership does not operate in a vacuum. It exists to achieve objectives which are set by the making of decisions and it is with the process of decision-making that this book concerns itself. Consideration, moreover, is confined to forms of rational decision-making. This is not to deny the existence or challenge the validity of other forms of decision-making based on emotion or intuition rather than reason but such forms, by their nature, have little of organised theory to support them. Rational decision-making, by contrast, is always rooted onto a conclusion, itself based on organised information which has been interpreted by some valid thought-processing technique.

Thought-processing techniques are of two distinct kinds. There are those to be used when the objectives set involve the operation of some fixed predetermined standard. These occur frequently in the use of familiar techniques such as Budgetary Control and Standard Costing or the setting of quotas for the Sales Force. The other kind of thought-processing technique is used when the objectives set involve optimisation as, for example, if profits sought are laid down to be the greatest possible and not merely some standard thought to be reasonably attainable. Examples of such techniques occur in the recently developed areas of Operational Research.

Preliminary to the application of a technique of either kind is the necessity to analyse the problem under consideration, identify the elements involved and, most importantly, measure them. Only then can a truly rational decision be reached because only then as Lord Kelvin has said, in a widely known and much quoted saying, can we begin to understand the problem. This is as true of marketing situations as of any other. Measurement adds depth to understanding as experience adds breadth to it.

It would be idle to pretend, of course, that measurement of all the elements in a situation is always easy. The attempt to measure should not be abandoned solely on that account. A conclusion is not necessarily of no value at all, if it is inaccurate, so long as due allowance is made for the inaccuracy when making the decision based upon it. Moreover, exact measurements are not always necessary. Often relative assessments are sufficient. The knowledge that Product A has a greater appeal than Product B, if a choice has to be made between the two, is sufficient even if no exact measurement of the appeal of either can be made. Care has to be taken to choose the most appropriate unit of measurement for the problem under study. The commonest unit is the financial unit and probably more often than not it will be the most appropriate one. It should not, however, be chosen blindly and without thought as to whether another might be appropriate. In many cases, actual quantities of goods sold give more insight into a problem than their value when prices of goods are variable.

The timing of the decision is of importance. Most marketing activities occur after the creation of the goods and services with which they are concerned. This is true for decisions concerned with providing goods at the right time and in the right place and partially also for pricing decisions. For decisions relating to the rightness of the product it is otherwise.

It is true that organisations do exist where the planning stage takes no account of marketing considerations. The product may be the result of research, say, and it is for those engaged in marketing to take the product as provided and handle it to the best of their ability. The marketing activity in such cases is product orientated. In most cases, however, the marketing activity is customer orientated, and marketing considerations must be brought into the picture at the planning stage before the product is created.

Measurement is normally thought of in numerical terms. Many of the conclusions reached in marketing decision-making are reached after the application of statistical or mathematical deductive techniques to the information available. On those occasions numerical measurements are necessary. There are other occasions, however, when the measurements need not be numerical and can be expressed in purely qualitative terms. Thus, for example, if market research establishes amongst consumers a preference for green and red as colours and production limitations decree that green and yellow are the only colours that can be provided, no numerical measurement is needed in order to reach the conclusion that the product to be produced should be coloured green.

Very often elements can be measured both in qualitative and quantitative terms. A rainbow, for example, can be described by listing its component hues in the order of the spectrum or by listing the wave-lengths of the colours. Indeed whenever the elements of a problem can be listed in some known sequence they can be given a crude numerical measurement by naming their place in the sequence. The letter F, for example, is the sixth letter of the alphabet and the letter Z is the twenty-sixth.

Listing the elements in a sequence is sufficient to provide the basis for some conclusions. Consider, for example, five elements A, B, C, D and E. If it is known that they can be arranged in the following sequence B, D, A, E, C where the value of some feature which they all possess increases from left to right, then some conclusions can be reached. In terms of their common feature C is better than E or B or indeed than any other and A is better than D or B. The conclusions can be reached that C + A is better than E + D or E + B and similar conclusions could be reached for other comparisons of combinations which are such that each member of one of the combinations can be linked with a member of the other combination which is known to be lower in the scale than itself.

Such a problem might face a caterer whose supplier could offer him a choice, say, of Dundee Cake, Madeira Cake, Digestive Biscuits, Abernethy Biscuits and Ginger Nuts arranged in that order of profitability with Ginger Nuts the most profitable and Dundee Cake the least profitable. Forced to decide between two products when he is restricted to handling only one, he can always decide which of the two is the more profitable for him by referring to the scale. Moreover, he can also always choose between say Dundee Cake together with Digestive Biscuits as against Madeira Cake together with Abernethy Biscuits, the latter pair being the more profitable since Madeira Cake is more profitable than Dundee Cake and Abernethy Biscuits are more profitable than Digestive Biscuits.

However, there are certain types of conclusion which cannot be reached. Would it be more profitable, for example, for the caterer to take Dundee Cake and Ginger Nuts rather than Madeira Cake and Abernethy Biscuits? Ginger Nuts are more profitable than Abernethy Biscuits but Dundee Cake is less profitable than Madeira Cake. With the information at present at his disposal it is not possible for him to come to a conclusion of this sort.

To be able to come to conclusions where the members of the pairs are not all always higher or lower than their opposite numbers an additional measurement is necessary. This is obtained by not merely measuring each element in terms of its position in the sequence but also by measuring its position against a scale. Referring back to the sequence of elements B, D, A, E, C it must be possible to say not just that D is more important than B and that A is more important than B but also, for example, that D is twice as important as B and that A is three times as important as B.

Some relative assessment must be made for each element in the sequence. If the assessments for E and C are that E is one and a half times as important as A and that C is three times as important as D the elements can not only be arranged in sequence but can each be given a scale rating. Thus they can be arranged as follows:

$$\text{Sequence B} \quad \text{D} \quad \text{A} \quad \text{E} \quad \text{C}$$
$$\text{Rating 1} \quad 2 \quad 3 \quad 4\tfrac{1}{2} \quad 6$$

Now it is possible to form conclusions not only about each individual element but about all possible combinations of them. For example, B + C scores 7 while D + E scores $6\tfrac{1}{2}$. If this general problem is translated back again into the caterer's particular problem, the conclusion he would reach is that Dundee Cake and Ginger Nuts is a marginally better combination than Madeira Cake and Abernethy Biscuits in the ratio $7:6\frac{1}{2}$.

Notice that the comparison should be expressed in the form of a ratio. It would be wrong to express it by saying that Dundee Cake and Ginger Nuts is half a point better than Madeira Cake and Abernethy Biscuits because the meaning of half a point depends on the unit of measurement being used. In this example the unit of measurement being used is the profitability of Dundee Cake since Dundee Cake has been assigned the rating of one. This might be an awkward unit of measurement like $7\frac{1}{2}d$. per lb or some such figure. The ratio $7:6\frac{1}{2}$ is a constant figure irrespective of the unit of measurement being used.

Notice also that it is not necessary to have exact values for the measurements. Relative assessments are all that is necessary. No doubt, in the case of the catering example, the absolute values of the profitabilities would be known. In other examples, particularly when dealing with matters of subjective judgement, absolute values could not be defined. This would not matter since all that is required is the relative assessment of each element in the problem in relation to the other elements.

Notice, finally, that once the problem has been defined and the elements measured, no marketing knowledge is needed to arrive at the conclusions. Marketing knowledge is certainly needed in order to specify the problem properly and to measure the elements sensibly. It is at this stage that the decision-maker uses all his experience of marketing and his specialised judgement. To proceed from that point to the conclusion is an exercise in reasoning only. What is required is the ability to deduce logically from the facts given. This is why rational decision-making can be done on a computer and, if the economics are right, should be done on a computer which is always the most efficient, if not always the most economical, means of making *logical* deductions from a set of facts.

It is stressed again that this is the case where the objective is to seek logical conclusions and to base rational decisions on the logical conclusions. The techniques which are to be described in the chapters which follow are all to be considered in this context. They do not necessarily apply if rational decisions are not being sought.

CHAPTER 2

THE RIGHT PRODUCT

To ENSURE that a product is *right*, in a marketing context, consideration has to be given to:

(a) the nature and quality of the product;
(b) the quantity to be produced.

The proportion of attention given to either of these two factors varies from organisation to organisation. In the case of public utilities supplying gas, electricity and water, for example, little variation is possible in the nature or even in the quality of the product. For them, the problem of identifying the right product is concerned mainly with settling questions about the quantity to be produced. By contrast, other organisations or professional individuals offering services such as building, dentistry or authorship are not concerned primarily with identifying quantity. Their problem is to make individual contact with a potential customer and, after discovering what exactly he wants, to negotiate a contract to meet his need.

The majority of organisations, however, are not monopoly suppliers of goods and services, nor are they in direct contact with individual customers. They have problems to solve relating both to the quality of the product and to its quantity. Answers to the first are sought by means of market research and estimates of the second are made using techniques of prediction.

The Function of Market Research

The function of Market Research is to obtain knowledge—knowledge of facts and opinions. Ideally perfect knowledge

8

can be obtained from the whole truth and nothing but the truth. In a marketing context this would require surveys conducted throughout the entire population by teams of investigators skilled in stimulating the responses of those interviewed and expert in distinguishing truth from untruth. This involves two practical impossibilities.

The first lies in the design and conduct of the survey. Practice and experience will go some way towards removing defects which will otherwise exist but operations in this field are still very much an art rather than a science. Measurement has little relevance at this stage of the market research function and this topic, therefore, lies outside the scope of this book.

The second impossibility, however, lies well within it. This impossibility lies in the fact that interviewers conducting a survey are not able to make contact with the entire population. Instead only a *sample* of those with knowledge to impart can, in practice, be interviewed. These partial responses form the basis of the conclusions on which decisions will eventually be taken.

If the feature on which information is sought were to occur in exactly the same way, whatever the event or whoever was involved, then the information obtained from any sample would be the same as the information that could be obtained from any other sample and each sample would exactly represent the whole. This unfortunately never happens. The environment surrounding each event or person, though in broad terms it may seem always to be the same, has differences in detail which produce differences in the characteristic under study. Moreover, outside a scientific laboratory, means of measuring characteristics are still relatively crude and there are always inaccuracies in the measurements obtained by market surveys. These influences give rise to *sampling errors*.

Sampling errors cannot be avoided but they can be understood. The decision-maker cannot hope for certainty in his information. Chance variations always occur but he can look for means of measuring uncertainty and take his decisions in the light of knowledge of the degree of uncertainty present.

The Workings of Chance

The problem is this. If the entire population gives rise to 100 observations of some feature under study and if there are no variations due to chance, then if a 10% sample is taken, it will not matter whether the sample consists of the observations numbered 1, 11, 21, 31, 41, 51, 61, 71, 81, 91 or the observations numbered 5, 15, 25, 35, 45, 55, 65, 75, 85, 95 or any other group of ten observations. All will give the same results and the results from any of the samples can be taken as representing the results of the whole hundred of the population. If, on the other hand, chance factors are operating then the results obtained from the sample of observations numbered 1, 11, 21, 31, 41, 51, 61, 71, 81, 91 will be different from the results obtained from the sample of observations numbered 5, 15, 25, 35, 45, 55, 65, 75, 85, 95. The likelihood is that no two groups of ten observations will give precisely the same results, nor is it possible to say which group best represents the whole population unless some means of measuring sample variations can be devised.

The questions that need answering are:

(1) Is it possible to get an idea of the range of variations in the observations resulting from the survey?

(2) Do samples of different sizes give different degrees of precision?

To get answers to these questions in a market research setting requires first a study of the operation of pure chance in a mathematical setting.

The operation of pure chance can be illustrated by considering what happens when one or several coins are tossed. When a single coin is tossed in a fair manner the chance that it will come down a HEAD is the same as the chance that it will come down a TAIL. If the coin was tossed 100,000 times the results would be unlikely to differ much from 50,000 heads and 50,000 tails. Half the results will be HEAD and half the results will be TAIL. There is one chance in two of getting a HEAD. This is expressed mathematically by saying that the probability of getting a HEAD is $\frac{1}{2}$. At the same time, of course, the probability of getting a TAIL is also $\frac{1}{2}$.

The results of tossing two coins are a little more complicated. There are these possibilities:

1st coin	2nd coin
HEAD	HEAD
HEAD	TAIL
TAIL	HEAD
TAIL	TAIL

If the order of tossing is of no concern HEAD-TAIL is the same thing as TAIL-HEAD. There is thus:

One chance in four of getting two HEADS;

Two chances in four of getting one HEAD and one TAIL;

One chance in four of getting two TAILS.

This can be expressed by saying that the respective probabilities are $\frac{1}{4}$, $\frac{2}{4}$ and $\frac{1}{4}$.

The ratio of the probabilities in the case of one coin is $1:1$.

The ratio of the probabilities in the case of two coins is $1:2:1$.

Similarly it can be shown that for three coins it is $1:3:3:1$.

And for four coins it $1:4:6:4:1$.

By examining all the possible results from tossing any other number of coins similar ratios can be found for any of them. The mathematician can derive these ratios by analysis and can show that the results can be obtained by giving different values to n in the *Binomial Expansion* of $(x + y)^n$.

The non-mathematician can derive these ratios in mechanical fashion by building up an array of figures known as Pascal's Triangle. In this array each row gives the ratios of the probabilities for tossing a given number of coins:

Pascal's Triangle

```
                              1
One coin                    1   1
Two coins                 1   2   1
Three coins             1   3   3   1
Four coins            1   4   6   4   1
Five coins          1   5  10  10   5   1
Six coins         1   6  15  20  15   6   1
Seven coins     1   7  21  35  35  21   7   1
   etc.                      etc.
```

Any number in any row is obtained, after inserting the figure one at either end, by adding together its immediate neighbours on either side in the line above. Thus in the row for seven coins the number 35 is obtained by adding together 15 and 20 from the row above.

These results can be shown in pictorial form in a series of histograms which plot the relative frequency of occurrence against the number of HEADS that might occur.

The histogram for the case of one coin is shown in Fig. 1.

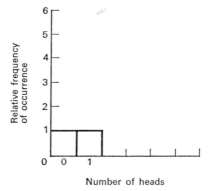

FIG. 1. Histogram for one coin

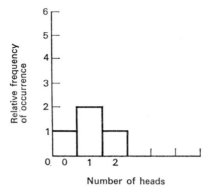

FIG. 2. Histogram for two coins

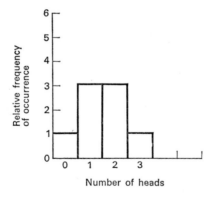

FIG. 3. Histogram for three coins

The histogram for the case of two coins is shown in Fig. 2.
The histogram for the case of three coins is shown in Fig. 3.
Similar histograms could be drawn for other cases. Figure 4
shows the case of 10 coins.
As the successive histograms for an increasing number of

coins are drawn, two features become increasingly apparent. These are:

(1) The symmetry round a central peak.
(2) The tailing away of the frequencies at the extremes.

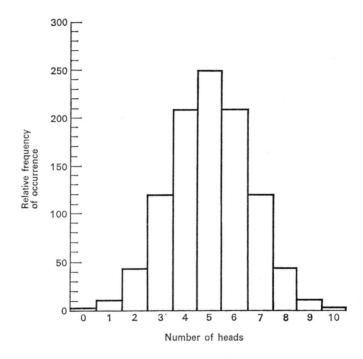

FIG. 4. Histogram for ten coins

As the number of coins increases the outline of the rectangles in the histogram approximates more and more to the appearance of a continuous curve. Ultimately when the interval between successive marks of the possible outcomes of the tossing is too small to distinguish, the frequencies are plotted as a continuous curve as shown in Fig. 5.

This is known as the *normal curve* and is one particular example of a *frequency curve* which, in turn, is a pictorial representation of a *frequency distribution*. A frequency distribution is a table linking the values that any observation or measurement under study can take with the number of times that value is taken.

In statistical work the quantity being measured is known as the *variable* and the number of times the value is taken is known as the

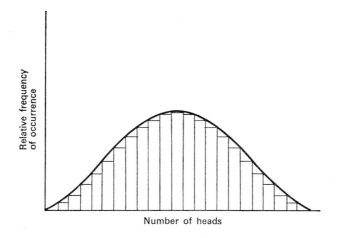

FIG. 5. The normal curve

frequency. The frequency distribution shows the frequency of each value of the variable. The results of market surveys constitute frequency distributions. If they were depicted graphically they might take up any shape. The normal curve is a very special case and it is unlikely that many market surveys would correspond exactly to its shape. However, as will emerge later, it does have an important relationship to sampling and for this reason its characteristics need to be known when attempting to use measurement for marketing purposes.

Measures for Dispersion

In practice decisions can not be based on every observation that is taken. The mass of data must first be reduced to a single measurement which can be taken to represent the whole. The simplest and most familiar representative is the *Arithmetic Average* and so long as there are no extreme observations from freaks in the survey which the decision-maker would wish to ignore, no great harm is done by using it. If, however, freaks are present and it is desired to leave them out of account other representatives can be chosen. One such is the *median* found by arranging all the observations in some appropriate and consistent sequence and taking as representative the middle of the array. Another is the *mode*, found by forming a frequency table and taking as representative the value of the variable which occurs most frequently. Expert advice from a statistician should always be obtained as to whether the set of observations being used is best represented by the arithmetic average, the median or the mode. It is nearly always possible, however, to transform, mathematically, conclusions based on the arithmetic average to conclusions which can apply to the median or mode. Indeed, in the case of observations which form a normal distribution the arithmetic average or mean, as it is frequently called, the median and the mode are one and the same representative. The discussion that follows, therefore, should be taken in the context that the mean is the chosen representative.

Whatever the representative, it is important to know how good the representative is—in fact, to be able to answer the first of the two questions posed earlier. That is, the one which asked "Is it possible to get an idea of the range of variations in the observations resulting from the survey?"

There are several ways of measuring the dispersion of observations. The crudest method is to take the highest value and the lowest value and to state the gap between them. Suppose, for example, a manufacturer of walking sticks is considering what is the best length to make his sticks. A survey is conducted for him and reveals the following preferences for walking stick lengths. The observations are displayed in a frequency table where the variable is the preferred walking stick length and the frequency is the number of persons who state a particular length as their preference.

FREQUENCY TABLE OF PREFERRED WALKING STICK
LENGTHS

Variable x (cm)	Frequency f
80	1
82	3
83	4
84	4
85	5
86	3
87	3
88	2
89	2
90	1

For this set of observations the choice of representatives lies between the

$$\text{mean} \quad = \quad 85\cdot07$$
$$\text{median} = \quad 85$$
$$\text{mode} \quad = \quad 85$$

If the manufacturer was working to very sensitive limits the difference between the value of the mean and the other two values might have some significance. One of the disadvantages of the mean is that its value may not be the value of any single observation. However, here let us suppose 85 cm is chosen as the standard length.

How good a representative is it? One way to describe its quality is to say that it is chosen from a range of lengths running from 80–90 cm. The practical interest of the marketing man in the measure of dispersion occurs when he wishes to market a range of products rather than standardise on a single product. The manufacturer in this case might notice that the observation of 80 cm was a bit out of line and since only one person in 28 had that preference he might conclude that he could ignore it.

He could ignore extreme measurements of this sort by using a measure of dispersion known as the *interquartile range*. This is obtained by dividing the set of observations into four equal groups and by ignoring the lowest 25% and the highest 25%. If this is done here, the interquartile range will be found to be 83–87 cm. The value of the interquartile range for marketing is that decisions taken to standardise on that range will have an appeal for 50% of the population.

Although these measures of dispersion are often used because of the ease with which they can be derived, their significance is difficult to determine mathematically when sampling is under consideration. For this reason a different measure of dispersion altogether is used and since very many marketing decisions are based on sampling, the marketing manager who aims to make rational decisions should become familiar with it.

Although at first sight this different measure of dispersion, which is known as the *standard deviation*, seems to be much more complicated than the others mentioned and much more difficult to calculate, in practice the steps to be taken are not difficult to understand. The procedure is as follows:

(1) Calculate the mean of the values of the observations.
(2) Calculate for each observation the difference between its value and the value of the mean. This difference is known as the *deviation* of the value.
(3) Form the squares of these deviations.
(4) Calculate the sum of the squares of the deviations.
(5) Divide the sum of the squares of the deviations by the number of observations to give a quantity known as the mean square deviation or *variance*.
(6) Take the square root of the variance to give the root mean

square deviation which, when the mean is being used as the representative, is known as the standard deviation.

Applying these steps to the observations of preferred walking stick lengths and setting the calculations out in tabular form, the

TABLE 1.

Variable	Deviation	Square of deviation
80	−5	25
82	−3	9
82	−3	9
82	−3	9
83	−2	4
83	−2	4
83	−2	4
83	−2	4
84	−1	1
84	−1	1
84	−1	1
84	−1	1
85	0	0
85	0	0
85	0	0
85	0	0
85	0	0
86	+1	1
86	+1	1
86	+1	1
87	+2	4
87	+2	4
87	+2	4
88	+3	9
88	+3	9
89	+4	16
89	+4	16
90	+5	25
		162

Sum of deviations squared = 162
Variance   = 162 ÷ 28 = 5·78
Standard deviation   = 2·4

standard deviation can be found as follows, if the mean is taken rounded off as 85 cm.

The significance of the standard deviation is that if the frequency distribution is reasonably symmetrical about a single peak, which means that it has a single mode, then it can be stated with reasonable certainty that two-thirds of the distribution lies less than one standard deviation away from the mean, that over 99 % of the distribution lies less than three standard deviations from the mean. For the marketing manager, this means that he has a method available for him to assess to what extent he has to widen his range of products in order to have an appeal to whatever proportion of the population he wishes.

The method of calculation has been shown in full detail in the example in order to illustrate the basic principle underlying the derivation of the standard deviation. In practice, there are two short-cuts which are usually employed.

The first is elementary and consists of avoiding the separate squaring of each of several values of the variable which are the same and adding the results. Instead the value of the variable is squared once and multiplied by the frequency with which it occurs. The second depends on a piece of mathematical manipulation. It can be shown by algebraic analysis that the variance can be calculated by taking the mean of the sum of the squares of the values of the variable and subtracting from it the square of the mean. The standard deviation is found by taking the square root of the answer.

The calculation is shown in the following table. The more exact value of 85·07 must be used for the mean.

To the level of accuracy used in the working this gives the same result as before. If more precise figures are needed it would have been necessary to take a mean of 85·07 in deriving the deviations in the earlier calculations. Although there are fewer steps to be taken the numbers involved are larger and a table of squares or some mechanical or electronic calculating device is desirable if the latter method is to be used.

TABLE 2.

Variable x	Frequency f	x^2	fx^2
80	1	6400	6400
82	3	6724	20,172
83	4	6889	27,556
84	4	7056	28,224
85	5	7225	36,125
86	3	7396	22,188
87	3	7569	22,707
88	2	7744	15,488
89	2	7921	15,842
90	1	8100	8100
			202,802

The mean $\bar{x} = 85 \cdot 07$
$\bar{x}^2 = 7237$
Variance $= \dfrac{202,802}{28} - 7237$
$= 7243 - 7237$
Standard
deviation $= \sqrt{6}$
$= 2 \cdot 4$

The Theory of Samples

The methods of interpreting frequency distributions which have just been discussed relate to situations where the information, though variable, is more or less complete and the possible courses of action open to the decision-maker are all known. The use of the concept of standard deviation was found to give a means of measuring the variability.

On many other occasions, however, the information is not only variable but incomplete and the courses of action open may themselves depend on the conclusions formed from the information. The conclusions will relate to the whole of the population covered by the decision but the conclusions on which the decision is based derive from information obtained from only a sample of the whole. If the move from conclusion to decision is to be as sound as possible, a knowledge of the behaviour of samples is desirable.

The simplest type of survey is the YES–NO type. This is used, for example, to measure the television audience for a particular programme. It is also used to discover whether or not a specified attribute of a product has an appeal. From the number who answer YES in the sample, an estimate is made of the number in the whole population who would hold the same view. This is done by assuming that the proportion of the whole population who would answer YES is the same as the proportion in the sample. The mechanics of reaching the conclusion is simple but to obtain a measure of the precision of the conclusion is not so simple.

The method of investigating variability is not available since in the sample there is only one measurement. However, the results from a *series* of random samples can be shown to form a normal distribution of their own and a standard deviation can be calculated for such a distribution. The standard deviation in the case of a sampling distribution is known as the *standard error* and it can be shown mathematically that in a YES–NO outcome if p is the probability of one outcome and q is the probability of the other outcome and n is the number in the sample then the standard error σ, is given by the relationship $\sigma = \sqrt{npq}$.

Suppose a television audience measurement reports that a sample of 1800 persons out of a total of 21,000,000 owners of television gives the record that one third of them watched a particular programme. The conclusion is therefore reached that 7,000,000 viewed that programme. The question is within what degree of tolerance should that figure of 7,000,000 be used in negotiations with commercial advertisers.

In this case, the standard error σ is given by taking $p = \frac{1}{3}$, $q = \frac{2}{3}$ and $n = 1800$ in the formula $\sigma = \sqrt{npq}$.

Hence $\qquad \sigma = \sqrt{1800 \times \tfrac{1}{3} \times \tfrac{2}{3}} = \sqrt{400}$

$$= \quad 20$$

When expressed as a percentage of the size of the sample this becomes

$$\frac{14 \cdot 14}{1800} \times 100\%$$

$$= 0 \cdot 785\%.$$

It will be remembered in connection with the normal curve that less than 1% of all observations occur beyond 3σ of the chosen representative. In this case $3\sigma = 1 \cdot 111\%$. Now $3 \cdot 333\%$ of 7,000,000 is 233,310. The conclusion, therefore, is that the true figure of those who watched the programme could be anywhere within the range 7,000,000 — 233,310 to 7,000,000 + 233,310 or from 6,766,690 to 7,233,310.

A rough and ready approximation to the standard error can always be found from the size of the sample alone and this approximation will always err on the safe side by exaggerating the standard error when it does not give it exactly.

Since $\sigma = \sqrt{npq}$, then for any value of n, σ will be a maximum when pq is a maximum. This occurs when $p = \frac{1}{2}$ and $q = \frac{1}{2}$ so the maximum value of $pq = \frac{1}{4}$. Hence the maximum value of σ is $\sqrt{n/4}$. In this example $n = 1800$ and it can be calculated that this gives a maximum value for σ of $21 \cdot 21$.

Expressed as a percentage of the size of the sample this becomes $1 \cdot 18\%$ and 3σ becomes $3 \cdot 54\%$. Hence an ultra-safe range for the number of viewers would be $7,000,000 \pm 247,800$.

This discussion of standard error has so far related only to the sampling of attributes. The survey in such situations asks only if such and such an attribute is considered to be present in the subject of the survey. The formula for standard error $\sigma = \sqrt{npq}$ when expressed as a proportion of the number in the sample becomes

$$\frac{\sigma}{n} = \sqrt{npq} \div n$$

$$= \sqrt{pq/n}$$

So long as p is reasonably large it will be seen that σ is small compared with p if n is large enough. So that if n is large enough, the error in taking the value of p obtained from the sample as the value for the whole population will be small. It can be shown that it also holds true when the sampling is not of attributes but of variables that so long as the sample is large enough there is little loss of precision in using as the mean and standard deviation for the whole population, the values of the mean and standard deviation obtained from the sample.

The phrase "if the sample is large enough" has been used more than once. It is not easy to say in advance of a survey just how large the sample should be. Once the results of the survey are known, of course, the standard error can be calculated and if it is considered to be too great the size of sample needed to reduce it to an acceptable value can be found. The cost of carrying out this additional survey can also be found and compared with the expected value of more precise information before any decision to proceed with the new survey is taken.

The formula $\sigma = \sqrt{pq/n}$ shows that the percentage sampling error varies inversely as the square root of the size of the sample. If it is desirable to halve the percentage sampling error, then it will be necessary to quadruple the size of the sample. If in the example just considered, the margin of error $3 \cdot 33\%$ is thought to be too wide for accurate decision making and that it should be halved, then this would necessitate taking a sample of 4×1800 or 7200 people instead of the previous 1800. Whether the cost of carrying out such a size of survey could be justified by the potential value of the decision based on the more accurate information would have to be considered.

By putting $pq = \frac{1}{4}$ into the formula $\sigma = \sqrt{pq/n}$ in order to give the maximum possible value of σ, a rough and ready way of estimating the size of sample needed to achieve any approved value of σ can be obtained by putting that value of σ into the equation $\sigma = \sqrt{1/4n}$.

Alternatively various proposed sizes of sample can be inserted into the formula to show what would be the maximum value of the sampling error.

Tests of Significance

In solving marketing problems an important need is to discover true cause and effect relationships. Does expenditure on television advertising produce more sales? Is it true that pipe smokers generally own dogs because if it is, then it might pay a manufacturer of pipe tobacco to advertise in kennel club journals? Large numbers of questions asked in marketing departments are of this sort.

Statistical results obtained by applying the rules methodically may often seem convincing but the interpreter of statistics must never lose the thought that even the most convincing results may occur by pure chance alone. He can never achieve certainty in his mind on this point but if he understands the workings of chance, he can estimate the probability of the effect he is observing being due to chance alone and not to some cause he has reason to believe is at work.

For example, when some new feature has been introduced into a product the marketing manager will wish to know whether it has produced any effect on the buying habits of his public. A survey will tell him what the new buying habits are and it will normally be the case that the pattern will be different from the old. But how significant are the differences? Are they really due to the introduction of the new feature and would they justify decisions concerning its retention? Or are they likely to have occurred by chance and to pursue them any further would be to pursue a mare's nest. A well-known politician has said that in politics pursuing mare's nests is an unfructuous operation. This is as true in marketing as it is in politics and what is needed is some method of testing the significance of the differences.

There are a number of tests of significance of which perhaps the best known and most straightforward in application is the *Chi-squared* test. This operates as follows:

(1) Set up data relating to the old situation before the introduction of the factor under study to act as a norm.
(2) Set up data relating to the new situation after the introduction of the factor under study.
(3) Calculate the differences between each item of the new data and its corresponding item of the old.
(4) Square each difference.
(5) Divide each squared difference by its norm figure from the old data.
(6) Sum the quotients so formed. This gives a value of χ^2.
(7) From published tables entered at the appropriate section for the degrees of freedom of the situation discover the probability of the differences being due to chance.

The greater the differences between the new and the old data the greater will be the value found and the smaller the probability of the differences being due to chance alone. The manager must then decide for himself whether the probability so obtained of the differences being caused by chance alone is sufficiently low to justify a belief that the new factor has indeed produced the change in the pattern. What constitutes a low enough probability is a matter of the circumstances of the problem and managerial inclination. Either a 5% probability or a 1% probability that chance only is at work is often taken as the significance level to be used.

Consider the coin-tossing example again and suppose a coin is tossed 1000 times. The expectation is that it will have come down HEADS on 500 of those occasions. In the event it is found that it came down HEADS on 650 occasions. Should trickery be suspected? How significant is the difference between 650 and 500 in this context?

The calculation is as follows:

Number of Heads expected	500	Number of Tails expected	500
Number of Heads observed	650	Number of Tails observed	350
Difference	150	Difference	150

$$\chi^2 = \frac{(150)^2}{500} + \frac{(150)^2}{500}$$

$$= \frac{22,500}{500} + \frac{22,500}{500}$$

$$= \frac{45,000}{500} = 90$$

Is this measure of the discrepancy 90 sufficiently high that it is unlikely to have occurred by chance.

By inspecting a table of values of χ^2 for different degrees of freedom the probability of that value of χ^2 having occurred by chance can be ascertained. This involves entering the table at the degrees of freedom appropriate to the situation.

The number of degrees of freedom of a problem is the number of classes of observation whose value can be assigned arbitrarily. In this case the number of degrees of freedom is one. This is, because of the two classes of observation;

(a) the number of heads; and
(b) the number of tails;

only one can be assigned arbitrarily. Once either the number of heads or the number of tails is fixed the other is completely determined. It must be the difference between 1000 and the first value.

For one degree of freedom the value of χ^2 at the 5% significance level is 3·84 and the value of χ^2 at the 1% significance level is 6·63. The value found is greater than either of these. In fact a value of 90 for χ^2 with one degree of freedom lies beyond ·001%. So that there is only something less than 1 chance in 10,000 that these results could have occurred by chance. More than that, the test cannot say. The decision-maker must make the final conclusion.

In a marketing context, suppose that the sales of seven brands of washing powder over the past year are known to have been as follows:

	Sales before campaign £ million
Dazzle	4·0
Whitex	2·0
Sparkle	1·4
No dirt	1·0
Spotless	0·8
Cleanall	0·6
Goodsuds	0·2
Total	£10·0

Three of these brands are controlled by one company and its subsidiaries. This company mounts a special advertising campaign for a month. At the end of the month it wishes to discover whether the advertising has had any effect in capturing a greater share of the market from its competitors. The sales for the following month are as follows:

	Sales after campaign £
Dazzle	330,000
Whitex	158,000
Sparkle	100,000
No dirt	88,000
Spotless	64,000
Cleanall	40,000
Goodsuds	20,000
Total	£800,000

To apply the χ^2 test, it is necessary first to calculate what might have been expected to be the sales if the pattern of market share had remained the same after the campaign as before it. The expected sales are then compared with the observed sales and χ^2 calculated from the differences according to the formula stated earlier. The calculations are as follows:

Shares of market previous to campaign are Dazzle 40%, Whitex 20%, Sparkle 14%, No dirt 10%, Spotless 8%, Cleanall 6% and Goodsuds 2%.

When these percentages are applied to the total sales of £800,000 obtained for the month following the campaign and the resultant figures compared with the observed figures, the differences are as shown in the following table:

	Expected £000	Observed £000	Difference £000
Dazzle	320	330	+10
Whitex	160	158	−2
Sparkle	112	100	−12
No dirt	80	88	+8
Spotless	64	64	—
Cleanall	48	40	−8
Goodsuds	16	20	+4
	£800	£800	NIL

$$\chi^2 = \frac{(+10)^2}{320} + \frac{(-2)^2}{160} + \frac{(-12)^2}{112} + \frac{(+8)^2}{80} + \frac{(0)^2}{64} + \frac{(-8)^2}{48} + \frac{(+4)^2}{16}$$

$$= 4\cdot79$$

In this case there are six degrees of freedom, because of the seven categories of soap powder six have values assigned arbitrarily but the value of the seventh is fixed as the difference between the sum of the six and the total. Entering a table of values of χ^2 on the six degrees of freedom line, it is found that the value of $\chi^2 = 4\cdot79$ lies at about the 60% confidence level, so that there is only about a 60% chance that the differences observed were the result of pure chance.

With an understanding of the workings of chance, the marketing decision-maker may prevent himself from jumping to false conclusions. He can never be given complete assurance that such and such is the case but he can be given an assessment of the probability that it is so. With this he must be content and it is for him to utilise the information to arrive at his best decision.

The topics discussed by no means exhaust the number of factors which can be considered in any investigation as to the rightness of the product. Not all the other factors are capable of being measured sufficiently accurately to justify as yet the development of deductive techniques for use in forming conclusions regarding them. One group of factors, however, concern the quantity of the product to be produced. The rightness of the product in respect of quantity may make all the difference between a company operating at a profit and operating at a loss. This is of such importance that much thought has gone into devising reliable measurements of quantity and these will be developed in the next chapter.

CHAPTER 3

THE RIGHT QUANTITY

MARKETING is not marketing unless the goods or services on offer are bought by a customer. Marketing decisions, therefore, must be based, at any rate in part, on what the customers want. In the last chapter methods of measuring the desires of customers were examined and assessed as to their precision.

Measurements of customer desires give only partial information. For one thing, the expressed desires may not be completely translated into action by the customer. For another, the organisation may not be able to meet the desires revealed to it. This may be because of deficiencies in its production ability or because of its inability to stand up to competition. Information on these aspects of the situation, which are vital to marketing decisions, come from past performance. Ways and means must be found of measuring past performance and techniques devised for interpreting the measurements.

It must be remembered, of course, that past performance is past and that the decisions to be taken relate to the future. The decisions, therefore, must give effect to thinking concerning the relevance of past information to the future.

In the absence of numerical measurements, qualitative epithets can always be used to describe past performance. Expressions such as the following will appear in the narrative of events:

"January Sales were poor. February and March showed an improvement while those for April were good."

Qualitative descriptions are not devoid of useful information. Statements such as the above provide a means of assessing relative performance. However, such descriptions lack precision. They provide no means of assessing the degrees of difference in the performances. Moreover, words like "poor" and "good" are subjective terms. They mean different things to different people.

Precision in Measurement

Precision is gained by using an absolute and objective scale of measurement. Thus, if actual values of sales are used as the unit of measurement, the statement can be revised to read

	Value of sales £000's
January	10
February	12
March	12
April	25

The *degree* of difference between the sales in the various months is now quite apparent. The choice of the words "poor" and "good" can be left to the individual interpreters of the sales results.

However, some further help can be given. The use of the words "poor" and "good" implies a comparison with some expectation and can only be justified if the basis of the expectation is specified. The statement of the sales results can, therefore, go further by giving, in comparison with the actual results achieved, the forecast of the results expected.

	Value of sales £000's	Forecast sales £000's
January	10	15
February	12	15
March	12	15
April	25	15

Now it is possible to see at a glance not only the degree of difference between the sales in the various months but also a measure of how "poor" January sales were and how "good" April sales were. The original plain language statement did not give any information on the quality of the February and March sales in themselves but now the performances in those two months can be seen also to have been not up to expectation.

Even if the original statement had been expanded to read "January sales were poor. February and March, while showing an improvement, still failed to come up to expectations. The results for April were good" there is still no information on how far the results in any month compared with expectation. Information of that sort is obtainable only if a yard-stick is incorporated and, to achieve precision, both the yard-stick and the measurements need to be expressed numerically.

In the tables given above and in most tabular statements of historical events, the measurement of each event is represented by a single value. It is important to realise that such a measurement reflects the result of the combined effect of a variety of causes. A decision taken now to apply in the future and based on these single values can be wholly valid only if the influences of each of these causes are the same relative to each other in the future as they were in the past. This, more often than not, would be a very dangerous assumption to make.

In order that a decision should be as sound as possible, an understanding of the way the major factors likely to be encountered can change their influence over time is necessary. Such factors fall into a number of broad categories. These are:

(a) short-term or local fluctuations;
(b) cyclical fluctuations;
(c) trends;
(d) chance variations.

When the influences of each of these factors has been allowed for, there will be left a residue of variations which are due to factors at present unknown or at best only half understood. To allow for them, the decision-maker has only his judgement to rely upon but before exercising his judgement he can and should ensure that the influences of the other factors which can be measured have been understood.

Short-term or Local Fluctuations

Short-term or local fluctuations are of frequent occurrence in business and are met at all levels of business operations. An ice-cream vendor plying his wares outside a school needs no telling that the numbers of potential customers varies with the time of day. The changing seasons bring their fluctuations and affect the sales of bathing costumes and umbrellas. Oysters are eaten only when there is an "r" in the month. Some fluctuations are geographical, bringing a greater demand for meat puddings in the North of England than in the South and, so it is said, making kidney soup more popular in Scotland than in England. Local fluctuations due to the distribution of income and wealth also arise. There is a greater concentration of Rolls-Royce cars in some areas of London than in others.

The influence of local or short-term fluctuations is obvious enough. Suppose the ice-cream vendor outside the school has a normal potential clientele of 200 customers and his marketing methods are sufficiently powerful so that his potential customers all become actual customers. Suppose that in addition two classes of thirty each visit this school from another school on Tuesday and Thursday of each week while on Wednesday one class of 30 go from the school for outside activity each week. The sales results for any week then will be as shown on page 35.

This gives a total of 1290 ice-creams in the week of six days from which he might deduce that in order to have a smooth pattern of production he should manufacture 215 ice-creams on each day. If he does so, there will be no single day on which his supply exactly meets his requirements. On Tuesday and Thursday he will lose business because his supply is exhausted before the

	No. of ice-creams bought
Monday	200
Tuesday	260
Wednesday	170
Thursday	260
Friday	200
Saturday	200

demand is fully met and on Monday, Wednesday, Friday and Saturday he has supplies left over which, if we assume he has no means of holding stocks over, will go to waste. On every day of the week his profits will be less than they might have been.

In this particular situation the means of acquiring information in order to improve matters is ready to hand. Moreover, the ice-cream vendor has been able to assume that without the major fluctuations referred to there was a constant market of 200 to which to apply the value of the fluctuations. But, even in this simple case, it is unlikely that the base figure of 200 will be constant day by day. There will inevitably be fluctuations due to absence of some of the children due to illness or some other cause. The ice-cream vendor could perhaps organise the flow of information from, say, the school janitor of the total number on the register each morning before he starts production. He might then go ahead and apply the corrections of adding 60 on Tuesday and Thursday and subtracting 30 on Wednesday to the figure of attendances on each of those mornings. If he did so he would still find that on many occasions he was wrong with his quantity manufactured because he would be wrong to assume that there were no absentees amongst the 30 leaving the school on Wednesday or that those coming to the school on Tuesday and Thursday were *always* 60.

Business situations are even more complex. Nor, in general, is it possible to get the information needed by direct enquiry or personal observation, although wherever possible these methods

TABLE 3.

	Monthly sales (£000's)												Total	Mon. aver.
	J	F	M	A	M	J	J	A	S	O	N	D		
1963	18	16	14	12	9	7	7	7	8	10	12	15	135	11·3
1964	16	15	13	12	10	8	7	7	9	11	13	16	137	11·4
1965	19	17	14	12	10	9	8	7	9	12	15	18	150	12·5
1966	19	17	15	13	11	9	9	8	10	12	14	17	154	12·8
1967	17	16	14	11	9	7	8	8	11	13	14	16	144	12·0
Totals	89	81	70	60	49	40	39	37	47	58	68	82	720	
Average (unrounded)	17·8	16·2	14·0	12·0	9·8	8·0	7·8	7·4	9·4	11·6	13·6	16·4	144	
Average (rounded)	18	16	14	12	10	8	8	7	9	12	14	16		

should be used. The information, more often, will have to come
from measurement of past performance and techniques have to
be found for disentangling the influence of local fluctuations and
applying the necessary corrections to reach reliable conclusions.

Consider the sales of a company as shown in Table 3.

The fluctuations in total business are minor and the company
is neither expanding nor contracting. On the other hand there are
seasonal fluctuations. Each year has the same general pattern—
high sales in winter and low sales in summer. To take the monthly
average calculated over the year as representative of any month
would be quite misleading. A measure of the modifications to be
made to the monthly average to arrive at meaningful monthly
figures is required.

A first approach would be to calculate the actual variations
on the figures available. If this is done, showing higher than
average sales as plus and lower than average sales as minus, the
following emerges for the year 1963 (Table 4).

TABLE 4.

	Deviation from mean (£000's)
January	+6·7
February	+4·7
March	+2·7
April	+0·7
May	−2·3
June	−4·3
July	−4·3
August	−4·3
September	−3·3
October	−1·3
November	+0·7
December	+3·7

If it could be assumed that the pattern of the seasonal variations
was precisely the same each year then these deviations could be
used to modify the expected monthly average for any year and so
produce the expected monthly sales figures. This assumption

TABLE 5.

	Deviations from annual mean (£000's)					
	1963	1964	1965	1966	1967	Average
January	+6·7	+4·6	+6·5	+6·2	+5·0	+5·8
February	+4·7	+3·6	+4·5	+4·2	+4·0	+4·2
March	+2·7	+1·6	+1·6	+2·2	+2·0	+2·0
April	+0·7	+0·6	−0·5	+0·2	−1·0	0·0
May	−2·3	−1·4	−2·5	−1·8	−3·0	−2·2
June	−4·3	−3·4	−3·5	−3·8	−5·0	−4·0
July	−4·3	−4·4	−4·5	−3·8	−4·0	−4·2
August	−4·3	−4·4	−5·5	−4·8	−4·0	−4·6
September	−3·3	−2·4	−3·5	−2·8	−1·0	−2·6
October	−1·3	−0·4	−0·5	−0·8	+1·0	−0·4
November	+0·7	+1·6	+2·5	+1·2	+2·0	+1·6
December	+3·7	+4·6	+5·5	+4·2	+4·0	+4·4

could not, in general, ever be made and the next approach, therefore, is to take the experience over a number of years and average the monthly deviations. If this is done for the five years 1963–7 the results are as shown in Table 5.

Taking the average deviations as shown in the final column and taking as base £12,000 which is the overall monthly sales figure for the whole of the period, a forecast of the monthly sales for 1968 could be made. This would be:

	Monthly sales for 1968 (£000's)
January	17·8
February	16·2
March	14·0
April	12·0
May	9·8
June	8·0
July	7·8
August	7·4
September	9·4
October	11·6
November	13·6
December	16·4

An alternative method of expression would be to show each monthly figure in the form of an index found by dividing the monthly figure as calculated above by the monthly average 12 and multiplying the result by 100. This gives then the following series related to the overall monthly average 12, as the base of 100.

SEASONAL INDEX FIGURES
(BASE: AV. MONTHLY AV. 12 = 100).

	Average	Index
January	17·8	148
February	16·2	135
March	14·0	117
April	12·0	100
May	9·8	82
June	8·0	67
July	7·8	65
August	7·4	62
September	9·4	78
October	11·6	97
November	13·6	113
December	16·4	137

If the monthly average remains constant or nearly so at £12,000 per month it will not matter which of the two methods of presentation are used for forecasting purposes. Both will give the same results. However, if the monthly average were to change year by year the question would immediately arise as to whether it would be reasonable to expect the absolute values of the deviation to be applicable irrespective of the level of the average itself. It might be suspected that to use absolute values would be to exaggerate the seasonal differences when the overall value was low and to minimise them when it was high and this would indeed be so. In such cases the index method is to be preferred.

This method of measuring seasonal influences has the merit of simplicity. It has a disadvantage if the figures are subject to a trend. This is because in calculating a simple arithmetic average as much importance is attached to the early years as to the later and when a trend exists this should not be so. Some means needs to be found whereby greater importance is attached to the experience of the most recent past rather than to that of years where the experience is much less relevant. This means lies in using a moving average rather than a simple average. The method is illustrated with the following figures which show a trend as well as seasonal fluctuations.

TABLE 6.

	Monthly sales (£000's)											
	J	F	M	A	M	J	J	A	S	O	N	D
1963	33	26	22	18	9	9	6	6	15	21	27	36
1964	36	29	29	25	12	9	9	6	18	24	24	42
1965	39	36	31	27	18	15	12	10	22	22	30	45
1966	43	38	35	31	20	17	14	12	24	24	33	48
1967	46	42	38	34	23	21	17	15	29	27	36	52

The first step is to take out a twelve-month total for 1963. This is 228. It is positioned in the middle of the year and since there are an even number of months in the year this will be between the months of June and July.

1963

—
—

May
June

228

July
August

—
—

Another twelve months total is then brought out for the twelve months ending 31 January 1964. This is calculated by adding to

the previous total the figure for January 1964 and subtracting the
figure for January 1963. In this case, this gives:
$228 - 33 + 36 = 231$. (This is positioned between July and
August.)

1963

—
—

May
June

228

July

231

August

—
—

A third twelve-month figure is similarly obtained for the year
ending 29 February 1964 and so on. These totals obtained in this
way are called *moving annual totals*. The moving annual totals
for the sales figures in this example are given in Table 7.

TABLE 7.

	Moving annual totals for sales (£000's)				
	1963	1964	1965	1966	1967
January		254	292	327	362
February		254	296	329	365
March		257	300	331	370
April		260	298	333	373
May		257	304	336	376
June	228	263	307	339	380
July	231	266	311	342	
August	234	273	313	346	
September	241	275	317	349	
October	248	277	321	352	
November	251	283	323	355	
December	251	289	325	359	

The next step is to calculate a twelve-month moving average by dividing each of the totals in turn by 12. The averages are positioned on the same lines as the totals from which they were obtained. This now results in the following (Table 8).

TABLE 8.

	Twelve months moving averages for sales (£000's)				
	1963	1964	1965	1966	1967
January		21·2	24·3	27·3	30·2
February		21·2	24·7	27·4	30·4
March		21·4	25·0	27·6	30·8
April		21·7	24·8	27·8	31·1
May		21·4	25·3	28·0	31·3
June	19·0	21·9	25·6	28·3	31·7
July	19·3	22·2	25·9	28·5	
August	19·5	22·8	26·1	28·8	
September	20·1	22·9	26·4	29·1	
October	20·7	23·1	26·8	29·3	
November	20·9	23·6	26·9	29·6	
December	20·9	24·1	27·1	29·9	

Next, an arithmetic average of the two moving averages on either side of a month is obtained. This is then positioned for the month in question. Thus for July 1963 the two figures on either side of that month are 19·0 and 19·3 giving an average, rounded up, of 19·2. The completed table is as shown (Table 9).

These averages are now transformed into seasonal index figures. This is done by dividing the sales figure for any month by the moving monthly average for that month and multiplying the result by 100. The results of these calculations are as shown (Table 10).

Finally a single set of seasonal index figures is obtained by taking an average of the four monthly seasonal index figures. This has the effect of ironing out the irregular fluctuations. The final index figures are, therefore, as shown in Table 11.

TABLE 9.

	Moving monthly averages for sales (£000's)				
	1963	1964	1965	1966	1967
January		21·1	24·2	27·2	30·1
February		21·1	24·5	27·4	30·3
March		21·3	24·9	27·5	30·6
April		21·6	24·9	27·7	31·0
May		21·6	25·1	27·9	31·2
June		21·7	25·5	28·2	31·5
July	19·2	22·1	25·8	28·4	
August	19·4	22·5	26·0	28·7	
September	19·8	22·9	26·3	29·0	
October	20·4	23·0	26·6	29·2	
November	20·8	23·4	26·9	29·5	
December	20·9	23·9	27·0	29·8	

TABLE 10.

	Monthly seasonal index figures for sales (£000's)				
	1963	1964	1965	1966	1967
January		170·6	161·2	158·1	152·8
February		136·8	147·0	138·7	138·6
March		136·2	124·5	127·3	124·2
April		115·7	108·4	111·9	109·7
May		55·6	71·7	71·7	73·7
June		41·5	58·8	60·3	66·7
July	31·2	40·7	46·5	49·3	
August	30·9	26·7	38·5	41·8	
September	75·7	78·6	83·7	82·8	
October	102·9	104·3	82·7	82·2	
November	129·8	102·6	111·5	111·9	
December	172·2	175·7	166·7	161·1	

TABLE 11.

January	160·7
February	140·3
March	128·1
April	111·4
May	68·2
June	56·8
July	41·9
August	34·5
September	80·2
October	93·0
November	114·0
December	168·9

In forecasting sales figures, the basic monthly figure is adjusted by the seasonal index to give the actual monthly forecast figures. The basic monthly figure must first be forecast. If there is no trend, the basic figure can be obtained from historical data and can be used as it stands. If there is a trend, however, this basic data must be adjusted to take account of it.

Correcting for Trend

The first step is to identify and describe the trend that has existed in the past and for which historical data exists. The simplest form of trend occurs when the amount of change in the figures is constant over each of the periods. Suppose sales are as given in the following (Table 12).

TABLE 12.

	(£000's)
1963	300
1964	330
1965	360
1966	390
1967	420

Here the amount of change is a constant £30,000 per year.

When figures for which the amount of change in each period is constant are plotted on graph paper the form of the curve joining them is a straight line. The word curve is used here as a mathematician would use it to mean the joining up of a set of points and this may be a straight line as here or curved in the more ordinary use of the word. The graph for the figures just given is shown in Fig. 6.

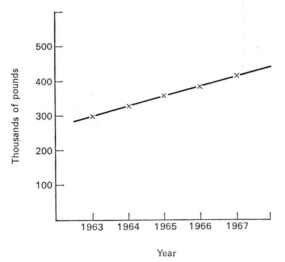

Year

FIG. 6. Straight line trend

It is rarely the case in a practical example drawn from real life that the figures lie so exactly on a straight line. Instead they are more likely to be represented in some such way as shown in Fig. 7 where the difficulty is that there is no single line which will fit all the points exactly.

It is possible to draw a number of lines all of which will give a reasonably good fit and the question is which is the one which gives the best fit. To be able to answer this question requires a knowledge of the mathematics of straight lines.

For the mathematician a straight line is defined by expressing the relationship between the various points in the form of an equation and he must find a means of identifying and describing the points which he wants to connect.

Any point on a surface can be described by giving it two reference measurements known as coordinates. A familiar example

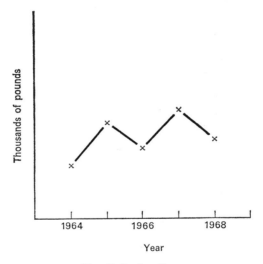

FIG. 7. Scatter diagram

is the use of latitude and longitude to describe a location on the earth's surface.

The mathematician similarly describes points by two reference measurements along two axes drawn at right angles to each other. The axis drawn horizontally is called the x-axis and the axis drawn vertically is called the y-axis. The intersection of the two axes is referred to as the *origin* of the reference system.

In Fig. 8, *O* is the origin, *OX* is the x-axis and *OY* is the y-axis. Both axes are marked out in appropriate scales. Any point can then be identified by giving its measurement from the origin along the horizontal x-axis and by its measurement along the vertical y-axis.

The point A is reached, for instance, by measuring 3 units along the x-axis and 4 units along the y-axis. It is written as (3,4). Similarly B is (5,8).

Any point can be identified in this way. Any description such as (3,4) or (5,8) or (a,b) where a and b might refer to any numbers

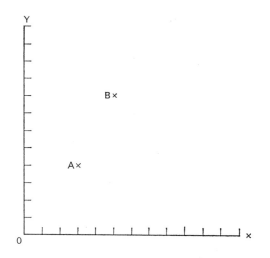

FIG. 8. Map references on rectangular axes

we like can each describe only one point. (3,4), for instance, uniquely describes the point A.

Although the point A can be uniquely identified by its coordinates this is not enough to identify any particular line running through point A. There is an infinitely large number of lines running through point A and to identify any particular one of them some additional piece of information is necessary.

Consider the particular line running through both point A and point B. It is possible to get from point A to point B by moving along the line A B and this will be the shortest distance between

A and *B*. Moreover, it is the only single straight line that can be drawn from *A* to *B*.

The coordinates of *A* are 3 along the *x*-axis and 4 along the *y*-axis while the coordinates of *B* are 5 along the *x*-axis and 8 along the *y*-axis. So as shown in Fig. 8, in moving from *A* to *B* the *y*-coordinate has increased by 4 units and the *x*-coordinate has increased by 2 units. For every unit of increase of *x*, *y* has increased by $4 \div 2 = 2$ units. This ratio of the increase in *y* to the increase in *x* is known as the *gradient* of the straight line *AB*. This is similar to the everyday use of the word gradient in measuring the slope of an uphill road, although for practical reasons the measurement of *x* is taken along the line of the road, along *AB* so to speak, rather than burrowing into the hillside. In mathematical use gradient is defined by taking the correct *x*-measurement. In this case, gradient is the difference in the *y*-measurements divided by the difference in the *x*-measurements and using the points *A* and *B* for both of which the coordinates are known, if *m* denotes the gradient

$$m = \frac{8 - 4}{5 - 3} = \frac{4}{2} = 2.$$

The gradient can be found by using any pair of points. Suppose there is a third point *C*, the value of whose coordinates are not known but it is known that *C* is a point on the straight line *AB*. In such a case the mathematician uses the letters *x* and *y* to denote the coordinates and the point *C* is therefore (x, y). Using *C* and *A* to measure the gradient,

$$m = \frac{y - 4}{x - 3}.$$

Since *AB* never changes its slope, the gradient must be the same whichever pair of points are used in the calculation. So

$$\frac{y - 4}{x - 3} = 2.$$

This can be rearranged to read

$$y - 4 = 2(x - 3)$$
$$= 2x - 6$$
or
$$y = 2x - 2$$

This relationship between any point (x,y) on AB and the point A is the equation of the straight line AB. It could have been derived by linking (x,y) with any other point on AB whose coordinates were known. It would have produced exactly the same equation.

Knowing the equation of AB it is possible to calculate the value of y which is linked with any value of x that is known. Its use in sales forecasting is that the values of x can be taken to be the time in years since the commencement of keeping sales data and y to be the value of the sales year by year. When the equation has been obtained by looking at the sales data it can be used to calculate the value of sales for any year past or future so long as it can be assumed that the same trend as appeared in the past will still appear in the future.

The generalised form of the equation of a straight line is $y = mx + c$ where m is the gradient and c is another constant. To find the value of m it is necessary to be able to define two points on the line and this can be done without drawing the line by inspecting historical data which in the case of sales forecasting will relate value of sales to the length of time that has elapsed since the data started to be kept.

If the data available identified points all of which fall naturally on to a single straight line the trend is easy to determine. Unfortunately data is rarely quite like that and, in practice, points can be identified which could fall equally well on to any one of a number of straight lines. The problem is to choose one of them which will represent the trend better than any of the others. How can this best fit be chosen?

Here the mathematician can be of help. If the horizontal axis of a graph is taken to represent the time scale and the vertical axis taken to represent the value of sales, then the data from historical sales figures can be plotted as a series of points for each of which the period to which the data refers is the x-coordinate and the value of sales in that period is the y-coordinate. It can be shown mathematically that the line of best fit passes through the point whose coordinates are the means of the two sets of measurements. If the mean of the time measurements is denoted by p and the mean sales figure as q then this point through which the line of best fit passes is (p,q). When one point on a straight line is known its equation can be written down as

$$\frac{y - q}{x - p} = m.$$

The value of m is the gradient of the line, and it has to be found before the equation can be finally known.

The method of finding the value of m is as follows:

(1) Find the middle time period of the data.
(2) Calculate a series of weighting factors for the data. The weighting factor for the middle period is O. The factors for the periods immediately before and immediately after the middle period are -1 and $+1$ respectively. The factor for the period two before the middle period is -2 and for the period two after the middle period is $+2$ and so on. If there is an even number of time periods the middle of the series will be midway between two time periods and the weighting factors will be $-2\frac{1}{2}$, $-1\frac{1}{2}$, $-\frac{1}{2}$, $+\frac{1}{2}$, $+1\frac{1}{2}$, $+2\frac{1}{2}$.
(3) Multiply the sales values in each of the time periods by its weighting factor paying attention to sign and add the results.
(4) Form the squares of the weighting factors and add the results.
(5) Divide the sum of the weighted sales values by the sum of the squares of the weighting factors. The result is the value of the gradient m.

The method is illustrated in this example. Suppose it is desired to find the trend in sales where historical data gives the following sales figures.

VALUE OF SALES OVER PERIOD 1953–1968

1953	2
1954	4
1955	10
1956	4
1957	2
1958	6
1959	12
1960	4
1961	2
1962	6
1963	12
1964	8
1965	4
1966	4
1967	16
1968	8
	104

The beginning of the year 1953 is taken as the origin 0, year 1953 is given the value $x = 1$, 1954 is given the value $x = 2$ and so on along the x-axis while the sales values are plotted as the y-values. So the point (1,2) denotes the sales for year 1953 and so on.

One point on the trend line can therefore be found to be

$$x = \frac{1+2+3+4+5+6+7+8+9+10+11+12+13+14+15+16}{16}$$

$$= 8 \cdot 5$$

$$y = \frac{104}{16} = 6 \cdot 5$$

The calculation for m can be seen from Table 13.

TABLE 13.

x	y	q	qy	q^2
1	2	$-15/2$	$-30/2$	225/4
2	4	$-13/2$	$-52/2$	169/4
3	10	$-11/2$	$-110/2$	121/4
4	4	$-9/2$	$-36/2$	81/4
5	2	$-7/2$	$-14/2$	49/4
6	6	$-5/2$	$-30/2$	25/4
7	12	$-3/2$	$-36/2$	9/4
8	4	$-1/2$	$-4/2$	1/4
9	2	$+1/2$	$+2/2$	1/4
10	6	$+3/2$	$+18/2$	9/4
11	12	$+5/2$	$+60/2$	25/4
12	8	$+7/2$	$+56/2$	49/4
13	4	$+9/2$	$+36/2$	81/4
14	4	$+11/2$	$+44/2$	121/4
15	16	$+13/2$	$+208/2$	169/4
16	8	$+15/2$	$+120/2$	225/4
Totals	104		$\dfrac{232}{2}$	$\dfrac{1360}{4}$

This gives $m = \dfrac{232}{2} \div \dfrac{1360}{4} = 0\cdot34$.

The equation of the trend line, therefore, is $\dfrac{y - 6\cdot5}{x - 8\cdot5} = 0\cdot34$ which simplifies to $y = 0\cdot34\,x + 3\cdot61$.

If it can be assumed that the trend as established is going to continue unchanged, the equation $y = 0\cdot34\,x + 3\cdot61$ can be used to forecast sales for any year. All that is necessary is to substitute the required value of x in the resulting value of y. If this is done for the years 1953–68 and compared with the actual figures as known, the results are as in Table 14.

If the divergences are examined it will be noticed that they go in cycles. Every fourth year actual sales as in 1955, 1959, 1963 and 1967 are very much better than forecast. A better measure of this *cyclical influence* is to express the divergence as a percentage of the forecast figure. The results of doing this are shown in Table 15.

Table 14.

	Sales figures 1953–68 (£000's)		
	Forecast	Actual	Divergence
1953	3·95	2	−1·95
1954	4·29	4	−0·29
1955	4·63	10	+5·37
1956	4·97	4	−0·97
1957	5·31	2	−3·31
1958	5·65	6	+0·35
1959	5·99	12	+6·01
1960	6·33	4	−2·33
1961	6·67	2	−4·67
1962	7·01	6	−1·01
1963	7·35	12	+4·65
1964	7·69	8	+0·31
1965	7·73	4	−3·73
1966	8·07	4	−4·07
1967	8·41	16	+7·59
1968	8·75	8	−0·75

Table 15.

DIVERGENCES AS PERCENTAGE OF FORECAST SALES

1953	−51%
1954	−7%
1955	+116%
1956	−16%
1957	−62%
1958	+6%
1959	+100%
1960	−37%
1961	−70%
1962	−14%
1963	+63%
1964	+4%
1965	−48%
1966	−50%
1967	+90%
1968	−9%

To evaluate the cyclical influence on the trend an average can be taken of the figures available for each of the years in just the same way as in evaluating seasonal influence. A seasonal influence is indeed a cyclical influence occurring within a time period of one year. If the figures in this example were those per quarter of a year instead of a year the variations would be those caused by seasonal factors. The calculation is as follows:

1953	-51%	1954	$- 7\%$	1955	$+116\%$
1957	-62%	1958	$+ 6\%$	1959	$+100\%$
1961	-70%	1962	-14%	1963	$+ 63\%$
1965	-48%	1966	-50%	1967	$+ 90\%$
Average	-58%	Average	-16%	Average	$+ 92\%$

1956	-16%
1960	-37%
1964	$+ 4\%$
1968	$- 9\%$
Average	-14%

These averages can be expressed as an index where the base is the figure of the trend forecast for each of the years in the four year cycle.

	Average	Index
Year One	-58%	42
Year Two	-16%	84
Year Three	$+92\%$	192
Year Four	-14%	86

With these two pieces of information, namely the trend equation and the cyclical index, a reasonable forecast figure of sales is obtainable. All such figures are still subject to error but an estimate of the probable error can be made using the methods described in an earlier chapter.

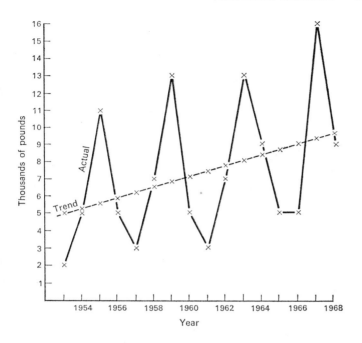

FIG. 9. Trend line and cyclical influence

Trend Patterns

(a) The trend pattern which has just been investigated is one in which sales alter by the same amount in each year. This is a pattern which can be represented graphically by a straight line. The practical interpretation of the trend equation is that the gradient m in the general equation $y = mx + c$ is the amount by which sales increase year by year and c is the level of sales at the point of time after which the sales data becomes available. In the example considered $y = 0 \cdot 34x + 3 \cdot 61$ the level of sales at the outset is taken to be $3 \cdot 61$ and the trend shows an annual increase of $0 \cdot 34$. Figure 9 shows the actual sales data plotted with the

M.T.M.—C

trend line superimposed from which the effect of the cyclical influence can be seen.

(b) Another trend frequently encountered occurs when sales are altering by the same *percentage* in each period. Table 16 shows the effect of such an increase compared with the effect of increases of equal amount.

TABLE 16.

	Values of sales (£000's)	
	10% increase per year	£30,000 increase per year
1963	300	300
1964	330	330
1965	363	360
1966	399	390
1967	439	420

When sales are subject to a *constant percentage increase* the amounts by which they increase period by period are now not constant but are themselves increasing. Figure 10 shows these two types of trend in graphical form.

The curve depicting a *constant percentage increase* trend is known as an *exponential curve* and its equation can be written down. Its general form is $y = ae^{bx}$ where a, e, b are constants. If the values of a and b can become known then the equation can be used for forecasting in the same way as the equation $y = mx + c$ could be used for forecasting constant amount increase trend. In both cases, of course, the assumption is made that the existing trend will continue. The value of e is always $2 \cdot 718$.

Calculations involving exponentials are not as simple as those involving straight lines. However, there is a special characteristic of this type of growth curve which provides a method of simplifying the calculations. This is the fact that the *logarithms* of the values lying on such a curve lie on a straight line.

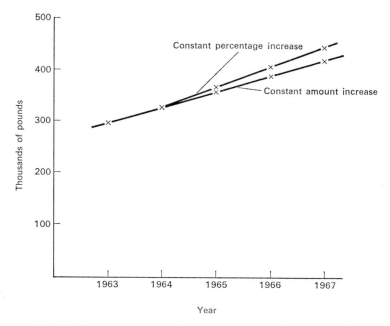

FIG. 10. Constant amount and constant percentage increase trends

The figures in Table 17 show this.

TABLE 17.

	Sales figures 1963–7	
	Value (£000's)	Logarithm of value (units)
1963	300	2. 477
1964	330	2. 518
1965	363	2. 559
1966	399	2. 600
1967	439	2. 642

It will be seen that correct to three places after the point the increase in the logarithms year by year is constant at 0·041. When these are plotted, as in Fig. 11, the result is a straight line.

If then the rules that have been developed for forecasting in straight line trend curve situations are applied to the logarithms of the sales values instead of to the sales values themselves, they can be used to forecast future sales so long as care is taken to

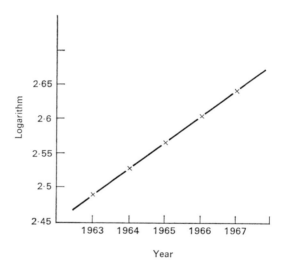

Fig. 11. Logarithmic straight line trend

remember to transform the logarithms back again to actual sales values after the calculations have been performed.

In practice, if the forecasting is done by graphical means the transformations can be looked after automatically. This is by using special graph paper, known as semi-log paper, in which the vertical scale is a logarithmic scale so that the sales values can be plotted as they stand without the necessity to look up the logarithms. Sales which change by the same percentage in each sales period, when plotted on semi-log paper, show up as a straight line.

(c) Constant volume increase and constant percentage increase trends are really applicable only when there is a single major factor affecting sales and other factors are considered to be insignificant. If they are not insignificant then other forms of expressing the trend have to be devised.

(d) Taking account of several factors requires a more complicated mathematical expression than those that have been described. The equation of a straight line which represents a constant amount of increase in the trend is the simplest form of what the mathematician calls a *polynomial*. The equation of the straight line $y = mx + c$ related y to terms which are either constant or are of a form containing x only. It does not contain terms involving x^2 (i.e. x multiplied by x). A term such as x^2 is referred to as being of *second* degree power because x appears *twice* multiplied together. A term involving x only is of *first* degree. A term such as x^n (i.e. x multiplied by x multiplied by x . . . to n factors) is of nth degree. The same descriptions are used for the equations. The equation $y = mx + c$ is a *first degree equation*. The equation $y = a + bx + cx^2$ is a *second degree equation*. The most general form of equation is one of nth *degree*, and is of the form

$$y = a_0 + a_1x + a_2x^2 + a_3x^3 + \ldots a_nx^n$$

where a_0, a_1, a_2, a_3 . . . are all constants. If there are a large number of significant influences on sales, then an equation of some higher degree than one might be used for forecasting purposes. Unless access can be had to a computer, however, the calculations involved with polynomials of more than second or third degree will be very time-consuming. For equations of low degree, however, the calculations may be tolerable.

The method used depends on certain facts about what the mathematician refers to as *differentials*, which are the rates at which the values of the variable under consideration are changing. In the case of the straight line relationship, the rate at which the sales were changing, it will be remembered, was constant. The rate at which the values change is known as the *first differential* and it is a mathematical fact that the first differential of a first degree equation is always constant. In the equation $y = mx + c$ the first differential is, in fact, m the gradient of the straight line.

For equations of higher degree than one the first differential will not be constant. The rate at which the first differential changes is known as the *second differential* and the rate at which the second differential changes is known as the *third differential* and so on. For an equation of nth degree it is the nth differential which is constant. For a second degree equation, therefore, it is the second differential which is constant.

How can this mathematical fact be used for sales forecasting? This can best be described by working through an example. For this purpose, suppose the sales trend can be represented by the equation $y = 15 - x + x^2$. This would express a relationship where, for example, an initial contract, signed with a small firm to under-pin it in the early days provided for an initial order of 15 to be followed a year later by an order for 14, and a year after that by an order for 13 and so on by further orders, the amount of the order reducing by one in each year. The unit in which the orders were expressed would be chosen appropriately to suit the particular circumstances. At the same time other business is expected to start small but to expand rapidly giving 1 at the end of the first year, 4 at the end of the second year, 9 at the end of the third year, 16 at the end of the fourth year and so on. The contract business can be expressed in mathematical form as $15 - x$ and the other business expressed in mathematical form as x^2. Hence the total sales are given by $y = 15 - x + x^2$. After the initial order of 15 sales will be as in Table 18.

The final column of sales in Table 18 is the starting point for the calculation of two further columns. These are the First Differences and Second Differences. The first differences are obtained by subtracting successive sales figures and the second differences are obtained by subtracting successive first differences. The results are shown in Table 19.

TABLE 18.
CALCULATION OF SALES FOR SEVEN YEAR PERIOD (UNITS)

Year x	Contract $15-x$	Ordinary x^2	Total $y=15-x+x^2$
1	14	1	15
2	13	4	17
3	12	9	21
4	11	16	27
5	10	25	35
6	9	36	45
7	8	49	57

TABLE 19.
TABLE OF DIFFERENCES

Year	Sales	First difference	Second difference
1	15		
		2	
2	17		2
		4	
3	21		2
		6	
4	27		2
		8	
5	35		2
		10	
6	45		2
		12	
7	57		

As will be seen the second difference has a constant value of 2 and if it can be assumed that the sales can be expressed mathematically in the same way in the future as in the past, this fact can be used to provide a forecast of the future.

To obtain a forecast for year 8, for example, the constant second difference 2 is added to 12 which is the last entry in the first difference column. The result 14 is then added to 57 which is the last entry in the sales column. This is then the forecast sales figure for year 8. The calculations for years 8 to 12 are shown in Table 20.

TABLE 20.
CALCULATION OF FORECAST SALES

Year	Sales	First difference	Second difference
		12	
7	57		2
		14	
8	71		2
		16	
9	87		2
		18	
10	105		2
		20	
11	125		2
		22	
12	147		

The table can be extended in this way as far as is thought desirable. In this example, allowance would have to be made at the end of the contract period for the fact that although sales under the contract would eventually cease they would not become negative. With this exception the method described can be used to give a forecast for whatever period it is felt sales will continue to be described by the expression $y = 15 - x + x^2$.

In practical work, the form of the mathematical expression will usually not be known. The difference columns can nevertheless always be constructed and one of these will often provide a reasonably constant difference figure. Using the method described each of the columns can be projected into the future and hence forecast sales. Alternatively the method of *multiple regression* can be used to identify the relationships between sales and each of a number of factors influencing sales. This method is similar to that previously described to identify a straight line trend for sales. The mathematics involved is, however, beyond the scope of this book and recourse should be had to some of the books mentioned in the bibliography for further reading. The methods described can be applied whether the trend is increasing or decreasing but are only valid on the assumption that the relative importance of the various influences on sales remain the same. It is often more realistic to assume, however, that some factors increase in importance while others decrease and to allow for this when making forecasts.

(e) One method of allowing for changing circumstances is to attach more weight to sales data relating to more recent experience than to sales data obtained from earlier years. Consider, for example, the crude prediction that because sales in the last two years have been 180 and 220 units, the sales during the next year will be 200. In reaching this conclusion equal weight has been attached to the figure of 180 as to the figure of 220. If it is known that circumstances changed after the year in which sales were 180, it would be more realistic to base the prediction more firmly on the figure of 220 than on the figure of 180. This can be done by weighting the figures before taking the average. If the weighting factors are $1:3$ then the average would be

$$\frac{1 \times 180 + 3 \times 220}{1 + 3} = \frac{840}{4} = 210.$$

In general a weighted average x can be calculated from the formula

$$x = \frac{a_1 s_1 + a_2 s_2 + a_3 s_3 + +}{a_1 + a_2 + a_3 +}$$

where $s_1 \, s_2 \, s_3 \ldots$ are the sales in years 1, 2, 3, etc., and $a_1 \, a_2 \, a_3 \ldots$ are the weighting factors to be applied to those years respectively.

The weighting factors to be used are a matter of judgement and experience. Certain patterns have been found to be realistic and useful in practice.

One such pattern is to allow the factors to form a geometrical progression, each factor being a given percentage of the factor immediately preceding it, taking the time scale backwards from the most recent year for which sales data is available. Suppose, for example, the ratio is 50%. Then taking a factor of 1 for the most recent sales data, the factor for the year immediately preceding it is 0·5 and the whole sequence of factors is 1 0·5 0·25 0·125 0·062 0·031 0·015 and so on for each of the years stretching back into the past from the present. This would be a very rapidly decreasing set of factors and would be tantamount to saying that the experience of earlier years was not very relevant to present judgements. A less drastic sequence would be 1 0·90 0·81 0·73 0·66 and so on where each factor is 90% of the preceding one. This concept of change by a constant ratio is the familiar one of the exponential curve. For this reason the technique is known as *exponential smoothing*. For practical working the calculations can be shortened by utilising the fact that each new weighted moving average can be found from the formula new W.M.A. = a × new sales figure + b × old W.M.A. where the factors have the relationship $a + b = 1$. It is only necessary to know for each year what factor a to apply to the new sales figure. The factor b is $1 - a$. The new weighted moving average is then taken as the predicted sales figure for the ensuing year. When the actual sales figure is known the next weighted moving average is calculated and used as the sales prediction. The following example illustrates the method. The weighting factors are taken as 0·5, 0·25, 0·125, 0·062, 0·031, 0·016, 0·008, 0·004, 0·002, 0·001.

Sales figures are available as follows in Table 21.

The calculation of the weighted moving average is shown in Table 22.

The exponentially weighted moving average is therefore 148·4.

Suppose now the 1969 sales in due course are known to be £128,000. A new exponentially weighted moving average can be calculated as in Table 23.

The exponentially weighted moving average is now 138·4. The same result could have been obtained more simply by using the formula new W.M.A. $= a \times$ new sales figure $+ b \times$ old W.M.A.

TABLE 21.
VALUE OF SALES (£000's)

Year	Value of sales
1959	146
1960	150
1961	118
1962	116
1963	138
1964	156
1965	124
1966	114
1967	142
1968	164

TABLE 22.

Year	Value of sales	Weighting factor	Weighted sales
1959	146	0·001	0·1
1960	150	0·002	0·3
1961	118	0·004	0·5
1962	116	0·008	0·9
1963	138	0·016	2·3
1964	156	0·031	4·8
1965	124	0·062	7·7
1966	114	0·125	14·3
1967	142	0·250	35·5
1968	164	0·500	82·0
			148·4

TABLE 23.
(£000's)

Year	Value of sales	Weighting factor	Weighted sales
1960	150	0·001	0·2
1961	118	0·002	0·2
1962	116	0·004	0·5
1963	138	0·008	1·1
1964	156	0·016	2·5
1965	124	0·031	3·8
1966	114	0·062	7·1
1967	142	0·125	17·8
1968	164	0·250	41·0
1969	128	0·500	64·0
			138·2

In this case $a = 0·5$ and so $b = 0·5$ also. The new W.M.A. therefore is found as follows:

$$\text{new W.M.A.} = 0·5 \times 128 + 0·5 \times 148·4$$
$$= 64 + 74·2$$
$$= 138·2$$

This method is of most use in forecasting for a very short period ahead where trends are of less importance than circumstances which have no consistent pattern. Where a trend exists the weighted moving averages will lag behind the actual sales but the pattern when allowance is made for the delayed effect will be the same.

In practice a combination of the methods described in this chapter should be used. For longer-term predictions other methods should be employed and these will be described in a later chapter.

CHAPTER 4

THE RIGHT PLACE

THE best products must in the end be placed in the hands of the customer. This involves two operations:

(a) creating a customer desire to have the goods or services which can be produced;
(b) physically ensuring the goods or services are in the right place for the customer.

Creating a customer desire is dealt with in a later chapter. Ensuring that the product is in the right place is considered in this chapter and has a number of aspects.

The first aspect is the type of channel through which goods flow from producer to consumer. There are two main types. One involves no intermediary between producer and customer, selling being direct or through sole agents. Familiar examples are the encyclopaedia or brush salesmen calling from house door to house door and the housewife agent of cosmetic companies taking orders in her own neighbourhood. The other involves one or more intermediaries between producer and consumer. These will include retailers, wholesalers and co-operative purchasing groups.

Many factors influence decisions on the setting up of channels of distribution and their operation. Not all of them are susceptible to exact measurement. One factor for which measurements can be provided arises in the consideration of choosing sites where contact can be made with customers.

Profitability

The fundamental measurement is, of course, profitability. Mere volume of sales is not enough since there is no surer recipe for bankruptcy than to expand sales of goods produced and sold at a loss. Profitability can best be expressed as a return on investment. If sales income is denoted by S and sales cost by C, then the

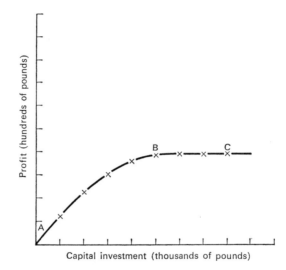

FIG. 12. Profit against investment curve

profitability measure is $100(S-C) \div I$, where I is the investment of capital required to produce the sales income S. The expected profit is $S-C$ and if this is plotted against I a typical graph would be as shown in Fig. 12.

Throughout the operations depicted by the part of the curve AB, extra investment produces extra profits. For that part of the curve BC, extra profits are not coming from extra investment.

There is little difficulty in deciding that investment should not go beyond B. Should it go as far as B? Not necessarily so, but reading an answer is not now such an easy matter. A measurement technique of value in tackling this type of problem introduces the concept of marginal costing.

From the graph in Fig. 12 it can be seen that although the successive increases in investment $X_2 - X_1$, $X_3 - X_2$, $X_4 - X_3$ are all equal, the additional profits $Y_2 - Y_1$, $Y_3 - Y_2$, $Y_4 - Y_3$ obtained from these equal packets of investment are not. $Y_4 - Y_3$ less than $Y_3 - Y_2$ which in turn is less than $Y_2 - Y_1$. Defining the extra profit $Y_4 - Y_3$ as the return obtainable from the last packet of investment $X_4 - X_2$ it will be seen that this return is very small indeed. This extra investment directed to another locality or in another operation might produce a greater amount of profit than $Y_4 - Y_3$. The total amount of investment desirable in any area depends on what this marginal profit is and it can be shown that the optimum allocation of resources to areas comes when an additional unit of investment yields the same profit increase in any area existing or contemplated. This concept of marginal costing is developed in detail in A. S. Johnson's *Marketing and Financial Control* published in the same series as this book and reference should be made to it for further knowledge.

Ranking of Sites

Not all the factors which go to influence the choice of sites for a store, say, will affect all the sites in exactly the same measure. It is rarely possible to devise an exact method of measuring the attractiveness of the various factors involved but it is possible to assess their *relative* attractiveness. Suppose it is considered that the following factors should be taken into account when reaching a decision as to which outlet in a locality should be used for a product, the factors being identified by the letters A to E:

A   Public transport facilities available.
B   Traffic congestion.

C   Reputation of the outlet.
D   Competitive goods available through the outlet.
E   Progressiveness of the manager.

Someone in the firm about to make the decision must seriously and rationally think out what degree of importance is to be attached to each of these factors. Inevitably subjective assessment must be made and this is where knowledge and experience and judgement count. These assessments can be graded on a scale of ten. Suppose for example "Reputation of the outlet" is considered to be the most important factor. This would be given a grading of 10. Suppose next it is considered that "Public transport facilities available" is the least important. This is not a sufficiently precise assessment. Judgement must be brought to bear to assess its relative importance compared with "Reputation of the outlet". Suppose it is considered to be only half as important. Then "Public transport facilities available" is given a grading of 5. Similarly the other factors are also graded and some such table as the following will emerge:

TABLE 24.

Factor	Grading
A	5
B	8
C	10
D	6
E	6

Now the possible locations for outlets must be listed. In this case the assumption is being made that only one outlet is either possible or desirable but this restriction is not essential and the method can easily be adapted to allow for the possibility of more than one location.

Suppose there are four possible locations:

1. High Street.
2. London Road.
3. Albert Square.
4. Victoria Parade.

Consider the High Street location in terms of attractiveness with respect to each of the factors influencing choice. Perhaps it is well served with public transport so that it ranks 8 points out of a possible 10. On the other hand it is a heavily congested traffic area and parking is difficult so that for this factor it ranks 2 out of 10 for attractiveness. The other factors can similarly be assessed, resulting in the following.

TABLE 25.
RANKING OF FACTORS

Factor	High Street
A	8
B	2
C	6
D	3
E	5

Each of the other locations can be assessed in the same way and a complete ranking table produced such as in Table 26.

TABLE 26.
RANKING OF FACTORS BY LOCATION

Factor	High Street	London Road	Albert Square	Victoria Parade
A	8	10	3	5
B	2	1	9	7
C	6	4	10	6
D	3	7	2	10
E	5	6	5	10

It remains to find some method of comparing these rankings objectively. To do this an index of attractiveness for each location can be calculated. The method consists of multiplying the ranking figure for each factor in each location by its grading in Table 24 and summing the results to produce an index for each location. For High Street, factor A has a ranking of 8 and the grading of factor A is 5 so that it contributes 40 to the index. The other factor contributions are similarly calculated. The calculations are shown in Table 27.

TABLE 27.
CONTRIBUTIONS TO INDEX OF ATTRACTIVENESS

Factor	High Street		
	Ranking	Grading	Contribution
A	8	5	40
B	2	8	16
C	6	10	60
D	3	6	18
E	5	6	30
Index			164

The complete table then becomes:

TABLE 28.
CONTRIBUTIONS TO INDICES OF ATTRACTIVENESS

Factor	High Street	London Road	Albert Square	Victoria Parade
A	40	50	15	25
B	16	8	72	56
C	60	40	100	60
D	18	42	12	60
E	30	36	30	60
Index	164	176	229	261

Victoria Parade has the highest index of attractiveness and therefore would be the chosen location if the choice were restricted to a single location, If the restriction were removed and any locations with an index greater say than 200 were permitted, then Albert Square would be used as well as Victoria Parade.

Such conclusions might require modification if the goods or services on offer were specialities. Customers might well then be willing to modify their normal behaviour and be quite prepared to travel long distances or put up with inconvenience in order to obtain them. In the extreme case of a firm possessing a monopoly of a vital necessity, it could no doubt establish its trading location wherever it chose.

Measurement of Trading Areas

Estimates of the size of trading areas can be made in a number of ways. Some of the most frequently used are:

(a) Audit of car index numbers parked in the vicinity of the chosen location.
(b) Circulation of newspapers.
(c) Examinations of customer addresses on invoices.
(d) Direct questioning of shoppers.

These measurements will give an estimate of the total area where inhabitants possess a propensity to shop in a particular location. They measure the net effect of all the influences at work.

Two of the principal influences on the choice a customer will make between two possible shopping centres are the total facilities available to him in each of the centres and the distances from his home to either of the two centres. Total facilities available in a shopping town have a close direct relationship to its population and distances are known from any gazetteer. In the U.S.A., W. J. Reilly has proposed a formula which states that the inhabitants of a locality with a choice of two shopping centres will divide in direct proportion to the populations of the two centres and in inverse proportion to the squares of the distances from the locality to each of the centres.

Thus, if P_a is the population of centre A
         P_b is the population of centre B
         D_a is the distance of the locality from centre A
         D_b is the distance of the locality from centre B

then, if the proportion of custom attracted from the locality to centre A is denoted by C_a and if the proportion of custom attracted from the locality to centre B is denoted by C_b,

$$\frac{C_a}{C_b} = \frac{P_a}{P_b} \times \left(\frac{D_b}{D_a}\right)^2$$

Consider, for example, Wellington, a town of 8000 inhabitants in the county of Somerset. Wellington is 7 miles from Taunton which has 37,000 inhabitants and 26 miles from Exeter, which has 92,000 inhabitants. If Exeter is taken as centre A and Taunton as centre B, and the appropriate figures substituted in Reilly's formula,

$$\frac{C_a}{C_b} = \frac{92}{37} \times \left(\frac{7}{26}\right)^2$$

$$= \frac{4508}{25,012} = \frac{18}{100}$$

So that for every 100 of the inhabitants of Wellington who went to Taunton, 18 could be expected to go to Exeter.

The formula can be used to determine the break-even point between two centres. This occurs where 50% of the custom going outside its own locality is attracted to each centre. It is found by putting $C_a/C_b = 1$ in Reilly's Formula. This gives

$$P_a/P_b = \left(\frac{D_a}{D_b}\right)^2$$

or

$$\frac{D_a}{D_b} = \sqrt{\frac{P_a}{P_b}}$$

Using this latter formula it would be possible to draw a series of contours round the various centres to give a map of the way in which the population in districts outlying the centres would divide their custom.

Reilly's formula is applied where the localities under investigation do not provide a full range of facilities. However, even a sizeable town which does provide a full range of facilities can be affected by the influence of an even larger town in the vicinity. The towns in the Southeast of England are all affected by London to quite a considerable distance from that metropolis. Some part of the trade of the smaller town will always be diverted to the larger. P. D. Converse, also working in the U.S.A., has adapted Reilly's formula to deal with such a case. The Converse formula is

$$\frac{C_a}{C_b} = \left(\frac{P_a}{P_b}\right) \times \left(\frac{4}{d}\right)^2$$

giving the ratio of custom from town B which goes to town A to the custom which is retained in town B.

d is the distance from town B to town A in miles
P_a is the population of town A
P_b is the population of town B

Neither Reilly nor Converse, in their formulae, attempt to differentiate between different classes of goods. Other formulae have been proposed which would allow for this but these are rather more sophisticated and beyond the scope of this book.

Shelf Space and Shelf Life

The most common forms of outlet are:
(a) small traders;
(b) multiple stores;
(c) department stores;
(d) supermarkets;

(e) door-to-door selling;
(f) automatic vending;
(g) mail order.

The major factor in determining the selection of one or more of these outlets is the size of the trading area and measuring techniques such as have just been described are of value in investigating them. However, other factors must also be taken into account.

One of these is shelf space. A supermarket or department store will have many products for sale, all competing for shelf space. On the other hand, the range of goods sold in smaller retailers will be very much less and products which are stocked have therefore less competition. The small retailer can not, of course, offer exposure to as great a number of customers as can the department store and the total amount of shelf space available will be less. However, a relationship may, by good sales activity, be more easily established with a small retailer which will allow to a product a greater proportion of the available shelf space than to its competitors and this will provide it with a greater prominence. How important this will be as an off-setting factor is difficult to determine in advance of events but the measurement of its influence is obtainable in the course of time from the rate at which the stock turns over. *Turnover* of stock is obtained as follows:

First, calculate an average inventory figure in units by adding the opening and closing inventory figures for the period and dividing by two;

Second, divide the sales measured in units by the average inventory measured in units.

Turnover figures should be calculated in this way for all goods and for all forms of outlet since they provide the means of measuring the performance of the final stage in the marketing operation. If resources are insufficient within the firm to do this thoroughly the aid of other firms providing this type of specialist service can be sought.

Connected with the factor of shelf space and stock turnover is the question of shelf-life. Modern methods of packaging and improvements in handling and storing goods have increased considerably the period during which most goods can be left on display. Nevertheless, particularly in the food trade, the question of shelf life is still of great importance. Goods left on the shelf too long are less than their best at the moment of sale and the discredit if not the fault rebounds to the manufacturer.

Measurement enters into the control of shelf life in two ways. One is by fixing a date beyond which the life of the product should not be extended. This will usually be indicated on the pack. The indication will be in plain language if it is intended that action should be taken by the customer himself in ensuring that no purchase of an outdated pack is made, or in code if such a result is primarily to be achieved by close selling supervision. The retail trader will in either event be encouraged to take out of his display goods which are no longer of sufficient freshness and representatives should be instructed to examine all stocks on each call to the extent necessary to ensure no old stocks get into the hands of a customer. If any such do get through the screen many firms guarantee free replacement.

Measurement enters into the control of shelf life also by fixing the frequency of call by the representative in such a way that the probability of finding outdated stocks is less than a tolerable amount. In the case of perishable foodstuffs or products such as cakes which quickly lose their freshness there may be daily deliveries by van salesmen. In less urgent situations the cost of making a call may be compared with the probable loss of goods after a given period and the frequency of call fixed by taking both into account. The achievement of a desirable amount of shelf space and the keeping of product waste to a minimum is brought about by frequent contact between manufacturer and trader. This is the work of the sales force and the size of the sales force is crucial to its performance.

Size of Sales Force

Before any reliable assessment of the size of the Sales Force can be made, a study should be carried out of the way a salesman spends his time. A salesman spends his time on many things: travelling, report writing, conferences are some of his activities in addition to direct customer contact work. All of them are necessary but only the direct contact work will produce the orders and the proportion of time spent on this must be established. Suppose it is 40%. If the working day is taken as 8 hours and the number of working days in the year as 240, then each salesman

has $\dfrac{8 \times 240 \times 40}{100} = 768$ hours per year available for selling time.

Not every contact will be an immediate customer. Experience and judgement will be called to aid to estimate the ratio of fruitful to all calls. Suppose 50% of all calls result in Sales.

Next it must be established what should be the frequency of call and what should be the length of call. These will be laid down as policy and will be different for different classes of customer. The following figures may be typical.

Customer class	Type	Frequency of call	Length of call
A	Single trader	Every 13 weeks	$\frac{1}{2}$ hour
B	Supermarket	,, 4 ,,	$\frac{3}{4}$ hour
C	Multiple Head Office	,, 2 ,,	1 hour

The total selling hours required can now be calculated.

Customer class	Actual customers	Total calls	No. of calls per year	Hours per call	Total hours
A	200	400	4	$\frac{1}{2}$	800
B	100	200	13	$\frac{3}{4}$	1950
C	10	20	26	1	520

This gives a total of 3270 hours. Since each salesman can contribute 768 hours per year the number of salesmen required is given by 3270 ÷ 768. This gives an answer of between 4 and 5. Hence the sales force must consist of 5 men.

An alternative approach is to consider the problem in terms of profit. Each salesman added to an existing sales force will increase sales volume. Initially, while the Sales Force is still small, this additional volume can be expected to be great, but after a certain stage of the build-up has been reached the Law of Diminishing Returns will commence to operate and the extra sales volume provided by the extra salesman will diminish. At the same time there will be for each extra salesman an extra expenditure incurred which is the cost of maintaining him in the field. With a proper costing system within the organisation it will be possible to identify the profit element in the sales income from the extra sales volume which is available to meet the extra expenditure. If this profit element is denoted by P and C is the cost of the extra salesman, the difference between the two is $P-C$. So long as $P-C$ is greater than nothing, it pays to continue the build-up of the sales force. If $P-C$ is less than nothing the sales force should be decreased. The optimum size of the Sales Force is reached with $P = C$.

The value of P depends on the size of the sales force and the volume of business. To determine the point when $P = C$ requires an approach using break-even charts and the concept of marginal cost to which reference was made in an earlier chapter. A fuller analysis of this form of measurement of the size of the sales force will be found in *Control of the Field Sales Force* by Douglas W. Smallbone, published by Staple Press, 1965.

Sales Territories

When trading areas have been measured and the size of the sales force has been determined, it remains to allocate territories to individual salesmen. This is no easy task and a policy decision must first be taken as to the principle to be adopted. The territories may be formed either (a) to ensure that each saleman has an equal potential for business and therefore for commission, or (b) to ensure that each salesman has the same work-load.

To attain either objective satisfactorily information is needed on

(1) the total market potential in all areas;
(2) the types of customer and their potentials;
(3) the forms of transport available;
(4) the distances between customers;
(5) the characteristics of each salesman;
(6) the efficiency of each salesman in terms of different types of customer;
(7) the efficiency of each salesman in terms of each product.

Information on the market will be obtained using the methods described in this and previous chapters. Information on salesmen is a matter of good sales management practice and although characteristics of salesmen are difficult to measure in precise terms measurements of their performances are available and can form the basis of assessments as to their relative efficiencies.

Before the advent of the electronic computer these factors were too numerous and too formidable for the decision-making techniques of the period to handle in any reasonable time. The use of an electronic computer does, however, bring the admittedly considerable calculations within the bounds of possibility. The technique of Linear Programming is one that can be used to work out sales territories taking account of numerous factors. The mathematics involved is too sophisticated to deal with here. It is described in managerial terms in *The Numerate Manager* by Fred Keay, published by George Allen and Unwin, Ltd. In practice, however, it is sufficient for the factors to be specified by the marketing manager and for the problem then to be handed over to the computer department or to a computer service bureau. The same technique has been successfully used in certain applications to determine the routes within territories of delivery vans. When related to salesmen's journeys it has come to be known as the *travelling salesman problem*.

Sales Control

After the strategy come the tactical decisions. The selling operations need to be controlled and their success or failure measured by a system of sales reporting. The basic data for all reporting is the performance of individual salesmen and the source is the salesman himself. This data is collected, summarised and presented in various ways to meet various requirements and these tasks will be performed by somebody other than the salesman or increasingly on a computer. The needs of individual firms differ in detail but certain fundamental principles of sales reporting are common to all.

(a) The simple sales figure tells nothing about performance. To do this it needs to be related both to time and the expected sales figure. The first need is achieved by regular reporting at standard intervals, usually weekly. The second by laying down budgets or quotas or at the very least by providing some previous performance as a standard of comparison.

(b) Information is needed not on the expected happenings but on the unexpected. Management by exception should be the accepted rule for sales reporting as for other management reports.

(c) The significance of deviations from the expected needs to be measured. Sales reporting is a basis for action and action should be confined to dealing with significant deviations.

(d) Information should be itemised only where separate decisions are needed for sections of operations.

Amongst the most commonly found reports are:

(1) A Journey Plan Sheet setting out for a period of time the areas for work for each salesman.

(2) A daily Call Report listing the calls the salesman makes and their category together with details of orders taken and other appropriate information on calls where no order is taken.

(3) A Customer Record Card recording the history of each customer.
(4) An Expense Claim Form recording outlays including car expenses.
(5) A Complaints Form recording details of dissatisfactions and complaints.

In the setting of sales targets there is little in the way of measurement techniques available. The judgements are largely subjective, making use of knowledge of individual salesmen's capabilities and working on information concerning the potential of the market. The level at which each quota is fixed depends, too, on the view held as to how quotas motivate the salesmen. Some managers fix targets at a higher level than is realistic not expecting them to be attained but believing that they act thereby as a spur. Others believe that the targets should be realistic because the satisfaction of a target attained provides the necessary encouragement for the future. Some agree the quotas with the salesmen themselves.

Assessment of performance within the organisation is not enough. Comparisons with the performance of competitors must also be made. Measurement here takes two forms. The first is the share of the market falling to the product of the organisation. A knowledge of this provides a means of deciding whether the growth shown by the internal controls is as great as it should be. The second form of measurement compares various ratios of performance with similar ratios of performance of competitors. Typical ratios are turnover figures and gross margins, net profits or any operating expenses expressed as a percentage of net sales.

In neither case will comparisons be obtainable with individual competitors but organisations exist to which a subscription will bring an assessment of performance relative to the general level of the industry. In return, of course, company performance figures must be provided under seal of confidence so that the comparisons can be made. Marketing in the right place just will not happen without sound interpretation of sound information.

CHAPTER 5

AT THE RIGHT TIME

THE chain of marketing activities stretches from the point of production to the point of sale. The length of the chain and the number of links in it depend on:

(a) the nature of the market;
(b) the nature of the producing firm;
(c) the nature of the product.

Customarily the links in the chain are:

Producer $\longrightarrow$ wholesaler $\longrightarrow$ retailer $\longrightarrow$ customer. Often, however, producers insert additional links by setting up warehouses of their own. This chain constitutes the distribution system for the goods being marketed. Correct decisions concerning the distribution system will ensure that goods are available at the right time.

Decisions concerning distribution systems are of three kinds:

(a) Those affecting the nature of the links.
(b) Those affecting the efficiency of the links.
(c) Those affecting the efficiency of the distribution system as a whole.

Some examination has already been made of the ways in which measurement can lead to decisions about the links in the chain. Most other decisions in this area of marketing are based on considerations which do not lend themselves easily to measurement.

Decisions affecting the efficiency of the links depend on two measurements. On the one hand it is necessary to know the costs both of those links in use and also of alternatives. On the other hand it is necessary to know how long it will take goods to travel the length of the distribution chain. Decisions based on these measurements take two forms.

The first form occurs when changes contemplated result in no increase in the time of transit. In such situations the decision-making process consists of taking out the costs of alternative courses of action. The choice will fall on the course of action which provides either the greatest absolute savings or the greatest return on capital. The technique of Discounted Cash Flow explained in most standard accountancy text books can be used with advantage to do this.

Conflicting Costs

Improvements in costs may, however, result in an increase in transit times or alternatively an improvement in transit times may be obtained only at the expense of higher costs. Decisions are required to resolve the conflict.

Consider, for example, a decision required to choose between air freight, rail freight or sea freight as a means of transport. The costs of these will be highest for air freight and lowest for sea freight. The transit times, on the other hand, are lowest for air freight and highest for sea freight. These considerations are pictorially shown in Fig. 13.

Increases in transit times may result in decreased sales and these must be expressed in terms of value. The decreases are the costs of slowing down the means of transport. Figure 14 shows the second curve added to the graph of the first.

The conflict arises because, although slowing down the means of transport reduces the direct cost, it increases the derived cost due to decreased sales. What is important for the decision is the combined cost curve obtained by adding the two costs. The combined cost curve is shown as a dotted curve in Fig. 15.

If a vertical line is now dropped from the lowest point of the combined cost curve to meet the *x*-axis at X, the point X will indicate the type of transport which should be used. For the type of transport thus determined, the combination of transport cost and cost due to decreased sales will be the lowest. At this point the marginal savings in freight from a slightly longer transit time would just equal the marginal costs of decreased sales.

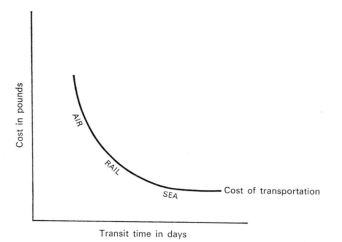

FIG. 13. Transportation cost and transit time curve

Inventory Control

In considering the efficiency of the distribution system as a whole, yet another factor has to be included. This is the possibility of holding stocks in warehouses at some stage of the system. Although introducing an extra cost, advantages arise from the opportunity to negotiate the more favourable transport rates applicable to larger loads and from the ability to make faster deliveries out of stocks to customers. Typical questions that now arise are the following. How many warehouses should there be? What stocks should be carried in the warehouses? The methods of

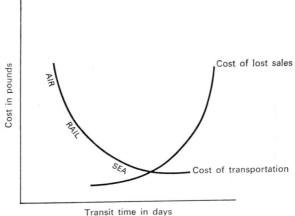

FIG. 14. Transportation cost, transit time and lost sales curves

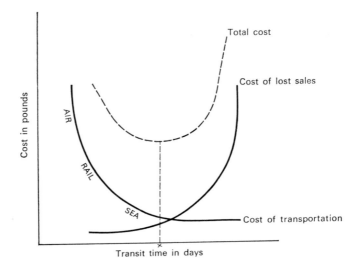

FIG. 15. Transportation, transit time and total cost curves

operational research are eminently suitable for the solution of such problems. The approach of the operational researcher can be illustrated by investigating a typical inventory situation.

The prime interest of the marketing manager is to maintain customer goodwill. To this end his concern is a high level of service and he will normally wish to ensure that all orders are met within a guaranteed delivery period. If he can forecast and control precisely for each period the orders he will receive, he can achieve his objective by maintaining an inventory at a level which will ensure that there are no stock-outs. His decision is based on these measurements:

(a) the inventory replacement lead time;
(b) the usage rate;
(c) the level of service to be provided.

Suppose the inventory replacement lead time is 5 days, the usage rate is 4 units per day, and it is desired to give a 100% service, that is all orders should be met from stock. Then the inventory level at which replacements should be requisitioned will be 20. Since the usage is 4 units per day it is known that when the inventory level is 20, stocks will be exhausted in 5 days time. However, the inventory replacement lead time is also 5 days so that just as stocks are exhausted, the replacement arrives. In this ideal situation, where usage is at a constant rate, the level of stock at which an inventory replacement should be requisitioned is given by the relationship

Ordering Level = Lead Time × Usage Rate.

How much should be requisitioned? This is again a conflict of costs. The conflict is between the cost of holding goods in stock and saving the costs of constantly requisitioning on the one hand and the cost of requisitioning with a consequent saving in stock holdings on the other hand. The problem could be solved graphically in the same way as was outlined above in considering the right choice for transporting goods. Here the curve that has to be drawn is the combined cost of placing a requisition for unit quantity and the cost of holding unit quantity in stock.

The solution can also be found by mathematical analysis. The elements of the problem are:

Q = requisitioning quantity in units,
C = inventory cost of one unit,
S = cost of making out a requisition,
U = usage during the period.

From these other elements can be derived:

$Q/2$ = average inventory,
U/Q = number of requisitions in a period.

The quantity held in inventory is Q at the commencement of a period just as the replacement quantity Q is delivered and reduces to zero just before the next replacement is due.

Hence the average inventory is $\dfrac{Q+0}{2} = Q/2.$

The total cost T is made up of the total requisitioning costs together with the inventory carrying costs.

$$T = U/Q \times S + Q/2 \times C$$

Using the techniques of the differential calculus it can be shown that this total cost T is at a minimum when

$$Q^2 = \frac{2US}{C}$$

or

$$Q = \sqrt{\frac{2US}{C}}.$$

This formula gives the quantity which should be requisitioned on each occasion in order to minimise the total costs of maintaining the inventory. It is valid where there is:

(1) a constant requisitioning cost per unit;
(2) a constant inventory cost per unit;
(3) a fixed demand;
(4) no quantity discounts;
(5) phased deliveries are not feasible.

Where these rather specialised conditions do not exist, the answers can still be found by applying the operational research technique of simulation. This proceeds by building a mathematical model of the situation, describing the elements of the problem and the relationships between them as a series of equations. The measurements may have to be expressed not as definite figures but in probabilistic terms and almost certainly a computer will be needed in order to solve the equations. The answers similarly require to be interpreted in probabilistic terms.

Patterns of Distribution

A further element in the cost of distribution is the transport charge that has to be borne in delivering goods from warehouse to customer. Transport costs can be high and thought given to the best pattern of distribution can be quite rewarding. Again the techniques of Operational Research and the speed and logic of a computer can give help.

Suppose there are five warehouses from which goods can be delivered to the four branches of a multiple customer. The costs in pounds per unit for each of the twenty routes along which it is possible to send goods are given in Table 29.

The capacities of the five warehouses are shown as 14, 8, 18, 8 and

TABLE 29.

| Branches | Total | Warehouses | | | | |
		1 14	2 8	3 18	4 8	5 12
A	18	4	14	6	4	10
B	8	2	12	12	2	10
C	18	4	10	4	6	14
D	16	6	10	2	4	14

12 respectively. The requirements of the four branches during the period are shown as 18, 8, 18 and 16 respectively. It is required to find the least expensive method of sending goods from warehouses to branches. Any plan must, of course, be subject to the restraints that no warehouse can supply more than its capacity and that each branch must receive its minimum requirements.

An experienced distribution clerk would certainly produce good plans but he could never know if he had hit upon the least expensive method unless he laboriously evaluated all the many thousands of possible alternatives. The technique of Linear Programming identifies with certainty that the least expensive distribution pattern is to send goods as follows:

To Branch	A	B	C	D
From Warehouse 1	0	6	8	0
From Warehouse 2	0	0	8	0
From Warehouse 3	0	0	2	16
From Warehouse 4	6	2	0	0
From Warehouse 5	12	0	0	0

If a computer is used the problem need only be stated for the solution to be found. All computers have standard programs for use on problems of this type. The manager must ensure that the problem is fully stated for no computer can ever fill in any gaps. In this context it is well to remember the cautionary tale of the long-service employee whose firm had over the years presented him with two gold watches. The first he had acquired after completing twenty-five years service, but this had long since ceased to go. The second he acquired after completing fifty years service, and checking this against a radio time signal found that it was losing 7 seconds in 24 hours. One day after receiving the second watch he retired. Faced with a reduced income it was decided that one of the two gold watches should be sold. His wife had no doubts as to which it should be but he had been so long in the computer atmosphere of his firm that he wished to put the problem to the computer. This he did and returned with the answer that the watch which should be sold was the one received yesterday and that the watch which should be retained was the one received twenty-five years earlier. Upon his wife insisting that some explanation should be obtained for this apparently absurd answer recourse was had once more to the computer. The explanation emerged that whereas the watch received twenty-five years earlier told the right time twice every 24 hours the one received a day or two ago told the right time only once every 18 years!

If the necessary condition of the problem was that the watch required to be working, this fact has to be stated. No computer can ever indulge in surmise and it will give a devastatingly logical answer to the problem as posed.

The translation of his problems into mathematical language need not concern the marketing decision-maker but the correct specification of his problems must be his concern.

Siting of Warehouses

The choice of sites for warehouses if costs of transport and operating vary from location to location is again a problem to be solved by Linear Programming. A simpler case arises when it can be assumed that unit costs of transport are constant and that operating costs do not vary according to location. Here the variable element is the distance from the proposed site to the centres of the population.

A method of solving this type of problem is to set up a pair of rectangular axes in such a way that all the centres of population fall between the two axes as in Fig. 16.

The intersection of the two axes is taken as the origin for all measurements. For each centre of population, two measurements are made, the distance eastwards from the origin (the x-measurement) and the distance northwards from the origin (the y-measurement).

Suppose these measurements for the n centres of population in

M.T.M.—D

the problem are x_1 x_2 x_3 . . . x_n and y_1 y_2 y_3 . . . y_n and the populations are p_1 p_2 p_3 . . . p_n respectively. A central warehouse should be located at the point $(a_1 b)$ whose coordinates measured from the origin are found as follows.

To find a, using the population figures as weighting factors, calculate the weighted values of the x-coordinates of the n centres of population and divide by the total population.

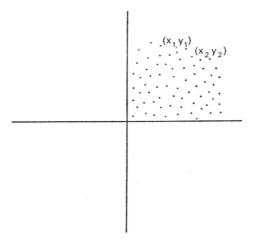

FIG. 16. Warehouse location reference diagram

$$a = \frac{p_1 x_1 + p_2 x_2 + p_3 x_3 + p_n x_n}{p_1 + p_2 + p_3 + + p_n}$$

Similarly, to find b, using the population figures as weighting factors, calculate the weighted values of the y-coordinates of the n centres of population and divide by the total population

$$b = \frac{p_1 y_1 + p_2 y_2 + p_3 y_3 + + + p_n y_n}{p_1 + p_2 + p_3 + + + p_n}$$

Suppose it is intended to set up a central warehouse to serve the following centres in the southern half of East Anglia:

Basildon
Chelmsford
Colchester
Cambridge
Bury St. Edmunds
Ipswich
Thetford
Southwold

Where should the warehouse be located? The calculation is shown in Table 30. All the figures were obtained from the AA Handbook for 1968–69, using the map on pages 20 and 21 and placing the origin at the intersection of grid lines Horizontal 8N and Vertical 4W. Measurements are in centimetres. There is some inaccuracy in assuming, as is being done, that the goods will travel as the crow flies. However, since the arithmetic can in any case only identify a general neighbourhood for the location of the warehouse the approximation is of no great consequence.

TABLE 30.

	p (000's)	x (cm)	y (cm)	px	py
Basildon	103	5·1	1·4	525·3	144·2
Chelmsford	54	5·0	4·2	270·0	226·8
Colchester	70	10·1	7·0	707·0	490·0
Cambridge	100	0·8	12·5	80·0	1250·0
Bury St. Edmunds	24	7·3	13·4	240·0	321·6
Ipswich	121	12·8	10·4	1558·8	1258·4
Thetford	10	8·2	16·5	82·0	165·0
Southwold	2	18·2	15·5	36·4	31·0
	484			3499·5	3887·0

$$a = \frac{3499·5}{484} = 7·2$$

$$b = \frac{3887·0}{484} = 8·0$$

A reference to the map reveals that these coordinates identify a point in the vicinity of Halstead which is therefore where a warehouse to serve the towns listed should be sited.

Providing Services

Many marketing situations involve the provision of facilities from which repeated services can be rendered. A check-out point in a supermarket provides the service of completing the customer's transactions. A store of spare parts provides the service of keeping the customer's purchase in good trim. A loading bay at the warehouse provides the service of speeding the products of the firm on their way to a customer. For a barber the chair provides the means of satisfying the customer's needs. A feature of all such situations is a queue of those requiring service formed at the point of service and involving for its members a period of waiting. The nature of the problem facing the manager is that of deciding on the facilities he should provide so that the time of waiting is not intolerable. Such problems are known as Queueing Problems and a technique of Operational Research known as Queueing Theory can be used to solve them.

The mathematics underlying queueing theory is beyond the scope of this book and the calculations are usually sufficiently involved to require the use of a computer. As always, however, when operational research and computers are in use the decision-maker must concern himself to ensure that the problem is correctly specified and measured.

It is first of all necessary to measure the elements of the Queue situation. Information is needed concerning the way arrivals add to the length of the queue, the pattern of attending to the needs and hence a decrease in the number in the queue, and the rules which govern the treatment of members of the queue. Such information will then be expressed in coded form if the data is to be processed on a computer or in the form of mathematical equations if it is to be processed by hand. In either case queueing theory provides the sequence of logical steps which have to be followed in order to deduce conclusions from the information provided.

The Application of Operational Research

Reference has been made to some of the techniques of operational research which can be used in marketing decision-making. In general a considerable knowledge of mathematics is needed to work out the solutions using such techniques and more often than not the calculations involved require the use of a computer. The non-mathematician is apt, in consequence, to fight shy of making use of such techniques. This is short-sighted and deprives him of valuable aids to decision-making. It is not indeed necessary for him to acquire an understanding of the mathematics but he should acquaint himself with the general characteristics of the types of problems which can be tackled using operational research.

These are of three kinds. First there are a wide range of decisions where the evaluation of possible courses of action and the interpretation of information can benefit by using standard mathematical procedures. Some of these were referred to in the discussion of sampling procedures in Chapter One. Second, there is a range of techniques known as *optimisation* techniques such as Linear Programming. These are useful in identifying the best course of action from a range of possible courses of action. The criterion by which "best" is to be judged must, of course, be defined. The third consists of simulating the situation facing the decision-maker by creating a conceptual model in mathematical terms and using mathematical procedures to reach conclusions concerning the situation. Queueing theory is one such example and other examples will arise in a later chapter when longer-term strategic problems come under discussion.

CHAPTER 6

AT THE RIGHT PRICE

IF AN organisation markets a near necessity for which there is no substitute and in which it has a monopoly, fixing a price at which to sell the product is comparatively simple. It consists of little more than identifying the costs of creating the product and deciding upon the amount of profit to add to the cost. Even in such a situation, nevertheless, there is a sanction which imposes a ceiling on the price to be charged. Above that level the customer will go without rather than pay the price.

In the case of non-essentials resistance comes at a lower level of price. Usually there are alternative products or competitors offering the same product. The price-fixer, therefore, must take account not only of the cost of providing the product but also of the reaction from the market.

For there to be a reaction at all there must be an awareness of the product, its nature and its qualities. It is the function of advertising to create this awareness and to the extent that it succeeds it influences the price at which the product can be sold.

There are then three influences on price. These are:

(a) cost of production;
(b) competition;
(c) advertising.

Costs of Production

Costs of production provide the floor below which price should not be allowed to sink. It is imperative that the full cost of getting the goods to the customer should be known. If there is a single product produced in a single pack that cost is identical with the cost of running the business. The total cost divided by the total number of units produced gives the amount that must be recovered in the price of each unit before any question of profit arises.

If the total cost C = £1,000,000
and the total product P = 750,000 units
then the price charged per unit must be at least

$$C/P = \frac{£1,000,000}{750,000} = £1\cdot3$$

When there are many products or several sizes of pack, difficulty arises in identifying just what are the costs of producing each product or each size of pack. Certain of the costs would not occur if particular products or packs were not being produced. These are *direct costs*. They can be isolated and therefore identified without difficulty. Other costs, however, would continue to occur even if particular products or packs were not being produced. These are *indirect costs* and *overhead costs*. Examples are the cost of the Engineering Maintenance Department and the cost of heating and lighting. Such costs cannot be isolated and identified as referring to any particular product or pack. Nevertheless, since the only source of income from which costs can be met is the income from the sale of the products, the price of every product and every pack must include allowance for some part of all indirect and overhead costs.

Methods by which this allowance is made tend to be somewhat arbitrary. There are five methods in common use:

(1) Application of overheads in proportion to direct labour costs. This assumes a direct relationship between overhead costs and direct labour costs. The result is that products with a high labour cost tend to be overpriced while those where labour has been reduced by the introduction of equipment tend to be underpriced.

(2) Application of overheads in proportion to direct labour costs and direct material costs taken together. The same distortions occur as when overheads are allocated in proportion to direct labour alone.

(3) Application of overheads in proportion to direct material costs by assuming a direct relationship with the weight of materials used.

(4) Application of overheads in proportion to units produced. Where products are closely related and output can be measured in terms of a common denominator this method is easy to use.

(5) Application of overheads in proportion to machine-hour rates. A machine hour rate is the cost per hour of processing the product in a production centre.

The choice of method can make quite a difference to the total costs identified for each product or pack and hence to the price which would be charged as can be seen from the following figures which determine the prices of two products, A and B.

	A	B
Production	4000 units	4000 units
Labour	£10,000	£20,000
Material	£20,000	£10,000

Overheads to be allocated total £12,000 and profit to be added is 25% of total costs. The prices that will result will depend on which method of allocating overheads is adopted. The calculations are shown for three methods.

Whichever method of allocating the overheads is used, the final result is the identification of all the costs. Profit must also be included. The simplest way of achieving this is to apply to the total cost figure a considered percentage of total costs as a *mark-up*.

A method of calculating this is to specify a required percentage

Overheads allocated in proportion to labour

		A £	B £
	Labour	10,000	20,000
	Materials	20,000	10,000
	Overheads	4,000	8,000
		34,000	38,000
	+25% Profit	8,500	9,500
		42,500	47,500
	Price per unit	10·625	11·875

Overheads allocated in proportion to labour and materials

		A £	B £
	Labour	10,000	20,000
	Materials	20,000	10,000
	Overheads	6,000	6,000
		36,000	36,000
	+25% Profit	9,000	9,000
		45,000	45,000
	Price per unit	11·250	11·250

Overheads allocated in proportion to materials

		A £	B £
	Labour	10,000	20,000
	Materials	20,000	10,000
	Overheads	8,000	4,000
		38,000	34,000
	+25% Profit	9,500	8,500
		47,500	42,500
	Price per unit	11·875	10·625

return on capital and from this calculate the mark-up using the formula:

Percentage mark-up on costs =

$$\frac{\text{Total capital employed} \times \text{Required return on capital}}{\text{Total costs}}$$

Contributions

A further distinction between different types of cost is necessary for a thorough understanding of the relationship of costs to price. Some of the costs will be incurred whether the product is produced or not. Others will be incurred only if the product is produced. These latter known as *out-of-pocket costs* are direct labour, direct material and direct overheads. When there is competition a knowledge of out-of-pocket costs is vital for pricing decisions.

The out-of-pocket cost determines the lower limit for price. For any lower price it would be more advantageous not to take the order and not to make the product. If competition would force down price to £100 while out-of-pocket cost is £110 a net outlay of £10 would be saved by not taking the order. For *any* price higher than the out-of-pocket cost there will be something available to meet the other costs of the business which would not be available if the order were not taken. The difference between out-of-pocket cost for a product and price is the *contribution* of that product. This contribution is available to meet the fixed expenses of the business.

To make any profit the total of contributions from all products must be greater than the total of fixed expenses. Even if this is not the case, however, it is still sensible to produce any product which can make a contribution. That contribution will reduce the loss from the level when the product was not produced. The level of sales revenue at which contributions are just equal to fixed expenses is the *break-even point*.

The amount of the contribution depends not only on the selling price but also on the quantity sold. Suppose the costs incurred directly as a result of production are £12 per unit. A selling price of £15 per unit will give a contribution of £3 per unit. If the quantity produced and sold is 3000 the total contribution is £9000. If a price reduction to £14 increases sales to 6000 the contribution will now be £2 × 6000 = £12,000. Thus, although the unit contribution is lower, the total contribution is higher and the firm is financially better off at the lower figure than at the higher, subject to one important qualification. This is that fixed costs remain unaltered in changing from one level of production to another. If additional equipment were needed, for instance, there would be additional depreciation and maintenance costs to include in the fixed costs. It would not then necessarily be true that the firm would be better off financially at the lower price than at the higher.

Elasticity

The sensitivity of volume sold to price is a very important concept. It is referred to as *elasticity of demand.* If the percentage change in volume is greater than the percentage change in price the demand is said to be *elastic.* If the percentage change in volume is less than the percentage change in price the demand is said to be *inelastic.*

The demand for necessities is inelastic. The demand for semi-luxury consumer durable goods is usually elastic. In practice, of course, it cannot be assumed that customers will behave consistently or that competitors will remain passive in the face of price-changes. Moreover, the way demand varies at a high price level may be different from the way it varies at a low price level. Again elasticity is not necessarily constant at all times and in all places. Nevertheless, in spite of the qualifications that must of necessity be made, a knowledge of the elasticity of demand at least in approximate terms is as important for determining prices as a knowledge of costs.

If e denotes the elasticity of demand, Q_1 denotes the quantity sold in a given period at price, P_1 Q_2 denotes quantity sold in an equal period at price P_2 then

$$e = \frac{Q_2 - Q_1}{Q_1} \div \frac{P_1 - P_2}{P_1}$$

If e equals one, proportionate changes in price are equal to proportionate changes in volume of sales. Price changes, therefore, will not affect Sales Revenue.

If e is greater than one, changes in sales volume are proportionately greater than changes in price. Sales revenue will increase as a result of a price reduction and sales revenue will decrease as a result of a price increase. The product has elastic demand.

If e is less than one, changes in sales volume are proportionately less than changes in price. Sales revenue will decrease as a result of a price reduction and sales revenue will increase as a result of a price increase. The product has inelastic demand.

Objectives of Pricing Policy

Pricing policy must be directed towards the achievement of objectives. Conversely, marketing objectives determine pricing policy. An objective may be any one of quite a number. Two of the most common are:

(a) to maximise the volume of sales and hence to capture the largest possible share of the market;
(b) to maximise profits.

If the marketing objective is to maximise volume of sales, costing information is used to determine the lowest permissible level for price. If there are no customer behavioural factors to take into account, this minimum price will be the price to charge in order to achieve maximum volume of sales. Before accepting this rigidly, however, care must be taken to ascertain whether customers react to the price of the product purely according to the laws of economics. Sometimes a low price produces non-economic reactions, a belief that the product is of poor quality, for example, or that it is shortly to be replaced by a new model and that price has been reduced in order to clear present stocks.

If the marketing objective is to maximise profits, costing information alone is insufficient. The mark-up must be such as to determine the price at which profits are highest, due regard being paid to elasticity of demand.

To date it must be admitted, there are few tools available for use in deciding upon an appropriate selling price. The difficulty arises in establishing the dimensions of demand. This is normally constantly changing. Normally, too, only rough assumptions can be made about its nature. The sensitivity of demand to changes in the economy generally and to marketing factors such as advertising, purchasing power, competition and good service, in particular, is not fully understood. Underlying these concepts is the whole diversity of human behaviour. Pricing decisions must therefore be based upon a sound analysis of market behaviour at the time a particular decision is to be made.

Market Research can help in providing an understanding of the underlying forces at work. In the absence of market research, experience may be the only guide and should, in any case, be be used to interpret the results of market research.

An alternative approach uses the rather more complicated mathematics of the differential calculus. It assumes that the quantity sold decreases in direct proportion to price increases. If q is quantity sold and p is price, this relationship can be written as $q = a - bp$ where a and b are two constants: a is actually the amount that would be sold if the price was zero and b is thea mount by which sales decrease for each unit increase in price. Similarly cost is assumed to be in direct proportion to quantity sold and is given by the relationship $c = l + mq$ where l and m are two constants, l being the cost incurred even when $q = o$ and m being the amount by which costs increase for each unit increase in quantity sold.

Total revenue is quantity sold multiplied by price or pq. Total profit is the difference between total revenue and cost. If total profit is denoted by z then $z = pq - c$. Using the formulae for q and c shown above and doing the algebra necessary, z is found to be

$$z = - (am + l) + (a + bm)\, p - bp^2$$

The techniques of differential calculus can be used to find which price will make the total profit a maximum. This is found to be the value of p which makes

$$a + bm - 2\,bp = 0.$$

The value of p which does this is given by

$$p = \frac{a + bm}{2b}.$$

To be able to calculate a figure for p it is necessary to make estimates of a, b and m, the significance of which was explained above.

This formula was derived using one particular pair of relationships linking quantity sold to price and cost to quantity sold. The method, however, is quite general and can be used for other forms of the relationships.

The conditions necessary for such an approach to be appropriate are:

(1) the period over which the policy is to operate is a stable period;
(2) the customer's reaction to price and cost are the only two factors of major significance;
(3) the equations for q and c can be considered as reasonably accurate.

An adequate costing system will enable the equation for costs to be stated. Historical data and market research must be used to establish the relationship between quantity sold and price and care is needed to ensure that historical data is suitably modified to take account of any changes occurring in the behaviour of customers.

Return on Capital

An excellent profit expressed as a percentage of sales may nevertheless be a very poor one expressed as a return on capital invested. A 20% profit rate on sales of one million pounds is only a 2% return on capital, if capital invested is ten million pounds.

The appropriate mark-up on cost to achieve a particular rate of return on capital invested can be calculated. The calculation depends on the fact that the percentage mark-up on cost multiplied by the cost equals the return desired on capital multiplied by the total capital employed. Both expressions define the total revenue that must be generated by sales.

If m is the percentage mark-up on cost

C is the total cost

r is the desired rate of return on capital

I is the capital investment

then $m \times C = r \times I$

$$m = \frac{r \times I}{C}$$ gives a formula for mark-up.

Multiple Products

When a number of products are marketed the objective is not to maximise the profit of any one product but to discover a set of prices which will produce the maximum profit for the whole product range. The issue is clouded by the cross-influences that exist between products in relation to demand and cost.

Cross-elasticity of demand is defined as the percentage change in quantity sold of product X for a percentage change in price of product Y. If two products are such that one can be taken in place of the other they are said to be *substitutes*. For example, an increase in the price of tea may increase the demand for coffee. Substitutes are said to have *positive cross-elasticity*. If, however, increased demand for one product increases the demand for another, the two products are said to be *complements*. A decrease in the price of cameras can be expected to increase the demand for films. Such products have *negative cross-elasticity*. If there is no relationship in demand between two products, they are said to have *zero cross-elasticity*. Cross-elasticities can be determined by the same methods as simple elasticities using historical data and statistical correlation techniques or by using survey methods.

Similar cross-influences often occur in costs of production; whenever there are by-products of the main production, there are such cross-influences. Equally, there are many cases where products will share some or all of the production facilities. The allocation of costs in all these examples is a matter for the cost-accountant and they must be made before decisions on prices are taken.

The combination of all these factors gives rise to a set of equations and conditions expressed in mathematical form and depending on the set of prices to be charged. The total profit can also be formulated mathematically. The problem is to find the set of prices which will maximise this profit function. This is a problem which also can be solved using the techniques of Linear Programming.

Advertising

The price mechanism manipulates the volume of sales under some particular conditions of demand. However, these conditions of demand can themselves be manipulated by advertising. The main question to be answered is the extent to which advertising should be used. Here the concept of marginal analysis is of value. In this context this states that expenditure on advertising should be taken to the stage where additional expense equals the profit from the additional sales caused by that expense. The subsidiary problems arise when the decision-maker tries to identify and measure the additional sales.

To be able to take measured decisions concerning advertising some understanding of the ways in which advertising produces sales is necessary. This understanding can come only from experience and it is at this stage of the decision-making process that sound judgement can and should be exercised. The commonly met method of settling the advertising appropriation by laying down that it shall be a given percentage of the expected values of sales is a method which is neither based on sound judgement nor attempts to measure.

Although fixing the advertising appropriation as a given proportion of sales is a simple procedure to operate, it is in fact putting the cart before the horse. Sales are the *result* of advertising and not its cause. In a period of steadily expanding sales it works well enough since advertising appropriations will then also be steadily increasing. When sales are dropping, however, advertising appropriations will be cut whereas, if there is any belief at all in the power of advertising to influence sales, they should be increased. Other similar procedures for determining the advertising appropriation such as taking a given percentage of the disposable profits or by fixing it in relation to the advertising appropriations of competitors are open to the same objection.

In order to build an adequate conceptual model of advertising operations the significant factors must be identified. The factors which are commonly the most significant are:

The rate of advertising expenditure.
The current rate of sales, giving a measure of goodwill.
The sales response factor.
The competitive threat.
The ceiling figure for sales.

The following illustrates the general approach. Suppose the marketing manager, using his experience and judgement, decides that his market share depends on:

(1) His current advertising appropriation.
(2) Delayed effects from the advertising appropriations of the two periods immediately preceding the current period.
(3) Brand loyalty as expressed by the market share held in the two periods immediately preceding the current period.

Suppose also that the marketing manager agrees that market

share is in direct proportion to each of the factors listed, that is that the relationships are linear. The model is built up in mathematical form.

Let a_1 a_2 a_3 be the advertising appropriations for the three periods concerned.

Let m_1 m_2 m_3 be the market shares for the three periods concerned.

If x_1 x_2 x_3 are the coefficients by which a_1 a_2 a_3 are multiplied and y_2 y_3 are the coefficients by which m_2 m_3 are multiplied then the equation $m_1 = a_1x_1 + a_2x_2 + a_3x_3 + m_2y_2 + m_3y_3$ enables the market share for any period to be found from the factors listed above, once values are known for the coefficients $x_1x_2x_3$ y_2 and y_3.

To be able to find values for them, five equations must be formed using historical data for market shares and advertising appropriations. Using algebra to solve the five equations the values of $x_1x_2x_3$ y_2 and y_3 can be found. Now, in the equation $m_1 = a_1x_1 + a_2x_2 + a_3x_3 + m_2y_2 + m_3y_3$ everything is known for the current period except m_1 and a_1. If a policy decision is made which lays down the market share which is desired this determines the value of m_1. The value of a_1 can now be calculated which gives the amount of advertising appropriation necessary to achieve the desired market share. The method is quite general and can incorporate any number of factors so long as the relationships are linear and sufficient historical data is available so that all the coefficients can be calculated.

Another type of model uses Linear Programming as the technique to achieve the solution. This determines not only the amount of the appropriation but also how it should be divided up amongst the various media competing for funds.

Suppose the problem can be stated as follows:

(1) The choices of media are:
      Television
      Daily newspapers
      Sunday newspapers

Monthly magazines
Quarterly magazines
and it is a matter of policy that all should be used.
(2) The maximum advertising appropriation that can be permitted is £500,000.
(3) For policy reasons the following spending limits are set:
at least £250,000 on television
at least £50,000 on daily newspapers
at least £1000 on each of the remainder.
What the reasons are does not matter, but they might be because it is feared that there would be no later opportunity to get back into a particular medium if it was, at any time, dropped.
(4) Exposures for each use are reliably estimated as follows:
300,000 for television
200,000 for daily newspapers
200,000 for Sunday newspapers
50,000 for monthly magazines
10,000 for quarterly magazines
(5) The costs per use are known to be
£15,000 for television
£10,000 for daily newspapers
£5000 for Sunday newspapers
£1000 for monthly magazines
£500 for quarterly magazines
(6) Any number of uses in a year is permissible for each of the media up to the maximum possible.

The objective of advertising policy must be defined. Suppose it is to achieve the maximum number of exposures. What, subject to the conditions laid down, should be the advertising appropriation and how should it be divided up?

If x_1 x_2 x_3 x_4 x_5 are the respective number of uses of each medium in order and the total number of exposures is denoted by E, then E can be expressed mathematically by the equation

$$E = 300{,}000x_1 + 200{,}000x_2 + 200{,}000x_3 + 50{,}000x_4 + 10{,}000x_5$$

All the conditions of the problem must be expressed mathematically.

(1) The condition that the total appropriation cannot exceed £500,000 becomes $15,000x_1 + 10,000x_2 + 5000x_3 + 1000x_4 + 500x_5 \leq 500,000$.

(2) The condition that at least £250,000 must be spent on television becomes $15,000x_1 \geq 250,000$.

(3) The condition that at least £50,000 must be spent on daily newspapers becomes $10,000x_2 \geq 50,000$.

(4) The condition that at least £1000 must be spent on Sunday newspapers becomes $5000x_3 \geq 1000$.

(5) The condition that at least £1000 must be spent on monthly magazines becomes $1000x_4 \geq 1000$

(6) The condition that at least £1000 must be spent on quarterly magazines become $500x_2 \geq 1000$.

(7) The condition that there may be any number of uses of television becomes $0 \leq x_1 \leq 365$.

(8) The condition that there may be any number of uses of daily newspapers becomes $0 \leq x_2 \leq 310$.

(9) The condition that there may be any number of uses of weekly newspapers becomes $0 \leq x_3 \leq 52$.

(10) The condition that there may be any number of uses of monthly magazines becomes $0 \leq x_4 \leq 12$.

(11) The condition that there may be any number of uses of quarterly magazines becomes $0 \leq x_5 \leq 4$.

The problem in mathematical form, then, is to find values of $x_1 x_2 x_3 x_4 x_5$ which will maximise

$$E = 300,000x_1 + 200,000x_2 + 200,000x_3 + 50,000x_4 + 10,000x_5$$

subject to the restraints

$$15,000 \ x_1 \geq 250,000$$
$$10,000 \ x_2 \geq 50,000$$
$$5000 \ x_3 \geq 1000$$
$$1000 \ x_4 \geq 1000$$
$$400 \ x_5 \geq 1000$$

$$0 \leq x_1 \leq 365$$
$$0 \leq x_2 \leq 310$$
$$0 \leq x_3 \leq 52$$
$$0 \leq x_4 \leq 12$$
$$0 \leq x_5 \leq 4$$

This will be recognised as a problem capable of being solved by Linear Programming. It can be fed straight into a computer and the result obtained in less than ten minutes. That part of the decision-making process is an automatic affair. The crucial part is laying down the plain language statement of the problem. Once that is done the problem can be handed over to the mathematician.

With sufficient thought, a mathematical model can always be created to describe an advertising situation. Where the model is based on linear relationships, methods for reaching a solution always exist. If the relationships are not all linear the method of reaching a solution may be quite complicated. Indeed in some cases there may not be a mathematical method of reaching the solution. However, this is for the mathematician and the computer expert to say. It is for the marketing decision-maker to ensure that *all* the elements and conditions of the problem are identified.

CHAPTER 7

STRATEGIC PLANNING

PROBABLY the majority of marketing problems are self-contained and short-term and the decisions required are tactical decisions for which the methods of measurement and techniques of deduction so far described in this book are suitable. There are, however, also marketing situations which are concerned with longer-term policy and which, far from being self-contained, have points of contact with many other functional areas of a business. Such strategic decisions must take account of the relationships that exist between the different facets of a business.

Consider, for example, the planning necessary for the introduction of a new product. The product has to be designed but the design cannot emerge in a vacuum. It must be related to the desires and likely responses of the potential customers. So the design department and market research come into contact right at the commencement of the project. Following this the product will have to be manufactured and the design cannot proceed very far without attention being paid to possible production difficulties. At some stage finance must be considered and the opinions of interested parties sought as to the capital investment involved and the likely return. All this is required before the more self-contained decision-making processes involved in settling questions of price, advertising or marketing.

An approach is needed which will see the problem in its entirety and which will bind the various facets of the situation together. At the same time it must provide a means of analysing the relationships that exist between the different sections of the problem and of reaching comprehensive conclusions.

Network Planning

Such an approach has become increasingly popular since its initial use in handling the complicated planning and scheduling necessary for developing Polaris in the U.S.A. Known originally as PERT (Progress and Evaluation Review Technique) it has become known as Network Analysis and includes now a number of variations of the original *Pert* concept.

The technique can be used for any planning project. It requires first that the project be broken down into its basic elements and the various stages in the progress of the project identified. The closeness of these stages varies with the level of management at which the planning is being done. At lower levels of management the stages are close together while at higher levels of management the stages are well apart. These stages are referred to as the *events* of the project and they are identified by reference numbers or letters.

Next, each event must be examined to see in what relationship it stands with every other event of the project. It will be found for any selected event that one or more other events precede it in the logical development of the project and that certain other events follow it. To move from one of two related events to the other some resource is used up. This may be material, labour, finance or time. The using up of a resource is referred to as an *activity*. The events and activities can be shown visually in the form of a network. In Fig. 17, the events are shown as circles and the activities joining related events as arrows, the arrow heads indicating the flow of the logical order.

The next stage of planning is to inject measurement into the description of the project. This involves estimating how much will be used up in each activity of the resource that is being controlled. When the estimates are of time, recourse can be had to the results of time studies or quoted delivery dates or past experience and in general, use must be made of all the means available in order to make the best estimates possible.

The method will be illustrated by an example. Suppose the marketing division is setting up a computer system to undertake their statistical work and planning is going ahead to have the appropriate computer programme prepared. The events of the project can be listed as shown in Table 31.

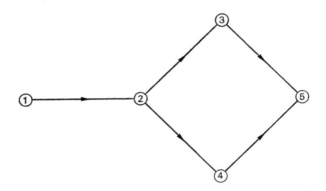

FIG. 17. Activity arrow diagram

TABLE 31.

Event	Description
A	Start of project
B	Computer order placed
C	Systems analysis completed
D	Systems flow charts completed
E	Programmers trained
F	Computer operators trained
G	Site prepared
H	Computer delivered
J	Programs written
K	Test data prepared
L	Program test begun
M	Program test completed
N	Program corrected

It is now necessary to consider very carefully how these events relate to each other and what are the activities that lead to each event and follow from it. For example, once event B (computer order placed) is reached, a number of things can flow. These are:

the training of the programmers leading to event E;
the training of the computer operators leading to event F;
the preparation of the site leading to event G;
the progressing of the delivery of the computer leading to event H.

The complete list of activities defined in this way is shown in Table 32.

TABLE 32.

Activities	Description
A–B	Preparing computer order
A–C	Doing general systems analysis
B–C	Doing specific systems analysis
B–E	Training programmers
B–F	Training computer operators
B–G	Preparing site for computer
B–H	Progressing delivery of computer
C–D	Drawing systems flow charts
D–E	Familiarizing programmers with flow charts
E–J	Writing of programs
F–L	Operator's preparation for program testing
G–L	Assembling of auxiliary equipment for test
H–L	Carrying out acceptance tests on computer
J–F	Familiarizing operators with programs
J–K	Preparing test data
K–L	Making test data available for program test
L–M	Carrying out testing of program
M–N	Correcting errors in program

If the resource to be controlled is time, as it is in a *Pert* network, the time each of these activities will take must be estimated. The unit of measurement will be the most appropriate unit for the

project. For mining operations it might be years, for heart operations in a hospital it is seconds.

Suppose the times are as follows, measured in some appropriate
unit (Table 33).

TABLE 33.

Activities	Time
A–B	4
A–C	5
B–C	2
B–E	10
B–F	7
B–G	10
B–H	52
C–D	15
D–E	4
E–J	5
F–L	1
G–L	2
H–L	4
J–F	1
J–K	3
K–L	5
L–M	3
M–N	1

The objective aimed at in applying Network Analysis in its
general form or using Pert, as in this example, is to supply answers
to three questions. These are:

(1) How long after the project starts will it be before the
program is ready?
(2) When can work on each of the stages start?
(3) Which parts of the project need the closest control?

The answers to the questions must emerge from the elements of
the problem. It is the purpose of the technique to make them
emerge. The first step is to arrange the identifying letters of the
events in some convenient sequence and then beneath each event

letter to show the letter of the starting event of each activity that leads directly to it. Thus,

A	B	C	D	E	F	G	H	J	K	L	M	N
	A	A	C	B	B	B	B	E	J	F	L	M
	B			D	J					G		
										H		
										K		

Next, at the right-hand side of each of the starting event letters put the time of the activity which links the starting event to the event being considered. Thus, under B goes the time for the activity A–B and under C go the times for the activities A–C and B–C. This results in Table 34.

TABLE 34.

A	B	C	D	E	F	G	H	J	K	L	M	N
	A4	A5	C15	B10	B7	B10	B52	E5	J3	F1	L3	M1
		B2		D4	J1					G2		
										H4		
										K5		

The earliest time each stage of the project can be completed can now be found. The steps of the operation are:

(1) Take 0 as the starting time of the project and show this value on the second line of the table, immediately under the letter A.

(2) Wherever the letter A appears as a starting event letter in the rest of the table insert 0 to the left of it.

(3) For every event which now has for *all* its starting event letters a value to both the left and the right of them the earliest time that can be reached is found by adding the left-hand figure to the right-hand figure for each of the starting

event letters and taking the largest sum. This is inserted immediately below the event letter.

The commencement of the table becomes

A	B	C
0	4	
	0A4	0A5
		B2

4 is calculated as the earliest time event B can be reached found from 0 + 4. The earliest time for C cannot be calculated since all the information is not yet available for starting event B under event C.

(4) Repeat the procedure until the earliest time has been calculated for each event.

Table 35 shows the result of these successive calculations.

The answers to the first two questions are now known. The program will not be ready until 64 time units after the start of the project and the earliest times each stage of the project will be reached are:

Event	Earliest time
A	0
B	4
C	6
D	21
E	25
F	31
G	14
H	56
J	30
K	33
L	60
M	63
N	64

TABLE 35.

A	B	C	D	E	F	G	H	J	K	L	M	N
0	4	6	21	25	31	14	56	30	33	60	63	64
	0A4	0A5	6C15	4B10	4B7	4B10	4B52	25E5	30J3	31F1	60L3	63M1
		4B2		21D4	30J1					14G2		
										56H4		
										33K5		

To obtain the answer to the third question as to which parts of the project need the closest control, a further set of steps is necessary. These work backwards from the end of the project, first of all showing under each event letter the letter of the end event of each activity that leads from it. This is shown in Table 36.

The steps to be taken now are:

(1) At the right-hand side of each of the end event letters put the time of the activity linking the event being considered to the end event.

(2) Take the final completion date, 64, as the start of this backwards moving procedure and show this value on the bottom line of the table immediately under the letter N.

(3) Wherever the letter N appears as an end event letter in the rest of the table insert 64 to the left of it.

(4) For every event which now has for all its end event letters a value to both the left and right of them the latest time permissible for that event can be found by subtracting the right-hand figure from the left-hand figure for each of the end event letters and taking the result with the lowest value. This is inserted on the bottom line.

(5) Repeat the procedure until the latest permissible times have been calculated for every event.

Table 37 shows the final result.

Examination of Table 37 shows that for certain events the earliest time that can be expected is the same as the latest permissible time. There is no slack to be taken up in those parts of the project. They are absolutely critical and need to be controlled rigidly. A path can be traced through the project linking the events with *zero slack*. This is the *critical path* for the project. In the example it runs:

$$A \to B \to H \to L \to M \to N$$

This critical path has another significance. If it is desired to improve the final completion date for the project, attention must be paid in the first instance to the activities along the critical path.

TABLE 36.

A	B	C	D	E	F	G	H	J	K	L	M	N
0	4	6	21	25	31	14	56	30	33	60	63	64
	0A4	0A5	6C15	4B10	4B7	4B10	4B52	25E5	30J3	31F1	60L3	63M1
		4B2		21D4	30J1					14G2		
										56H4		
										33K5		

B	C	D	E	F	G	H	J	K	L	M
C	D	E	J	L	L	L	F	L	M	N
E							K			
F										
G										
H										

TABLE 37.

A	B	C	D	E	F	G	H	J	K	L	M	N
0	4 0A4	6 0A5 4B2	21 6C15	25 4B10 21D4	31 4B7 30J1	14 4B10	56 4B52	30 25E5	33 30J3	60 31F1 14G2 56H4 33K5	63 60L3	64 63M1
4B4 33C5	33C2 52E10 59F7 58G10 56H52	43D15	47E4	52J5	60L1	60L2	60L4	59F1 55K3	60L5	63M3	64N1	
0	4	28	43	47	59	58	56	52	55	60	63	64

If no improvement can be made in the activities along the critical path then no improvement can be made to the final completion date no matter what is done in other parts of the project.

Table 37 shows not only the events of zero slack which lie on the critical path but shows also what spare time there is at every other

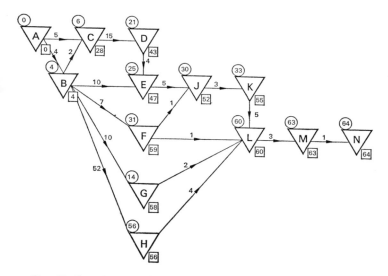

FIG. 18. Completed arrow diagram (reproduced from *The Numerate Manager* by Fred Keay, published by Geo. Allen and Unwin Ltd.)

stage of the project. This spare time is the difference between the earliest time that can be expected for an event and the latest permissible time for it. A knowledge of what time is spare at each stage of the project is of great importance in scheduling resources.

The determination of the critical path is more commonly effected by a visual representation as was indicated at the commencement of the description of this technique. The final diagram for the example worked out is shown in Fig. 18.

Figure 18 is, of course, Table 37 in visual form. Which method is adopted is a matter of preference. The visual method is the one usually described in the textbooks of which some are listed in the bibliography at the end of this book.

Choosing the Measurements

The conclusions reached in any of the forms of network planning will be governed by the measurements that are used as well as by the relationships between different parts of the problem. Varying estimates of these measurements may be forthcoming from different sources and for ease in working these will have to be condensed into a single measurement. This will apply whatever the resource that is being measured.

A statistical means of obtaining a single measurement is commonly used. Three measurements are first obtained.

(1) That which would apply if all circumstances were at their *most* favourable.
(2) That which would apply if all circumstances were at their *least* favourable.
(3) That which is thought to be the most probable.

These three measurements can be considered as the Optimistic Measurement, the Pessimistic Measurement and the Realistic Measurement and can be denoted as Q_o, Q_p and Q_r and they can be combined to give a single measurement

$$Q = \frac{Q_o + 4Q_r + Q_p}{6}.$$

The statistical significance of this calculated value of the measurement is that there is a 50 % chance that in practice the true value of the measurement will turn out to be greater than Q and a 50 % chance that in practice the actual value will turn out to be less than Q.

To some, such a statistical measurement may seem a little artificial. They may prefer to rely on subjective assessments of the realistic time only because these will be based on the experience and judgement of those best qualified to advise. These will vary, of course, but they can still be combined into a single measurement by taking the median or the mode of the separate measurements.

Measurement of Uncertainty

Whatever method is used for obtaining a measurement there will always be some error involved. This cannot be avoided although, of course, all steps should be taken to minimise it. That there will be uncertainty in the conclusions drawn from the measurements has to be accepted but it is defeatist to take the view that the process of reaching the conclusions is invalid as a result. It is possible to understand the nature and the extent of the uncertainty in the conclusions. There are two main ways in which this is done: first by considering what happens when measurements are added together and secondly what happens when two measurements are multiplied together.

Suppose the sales forecast for the first quarter of 1970 is 10,000 units but the Sales Manager responsible estimates that he might be 1000 units out in either direction. This means that the real sales may turn out to be anything from 9000 units to 11,000 units. Similarly, the sales forecast for the second quarter is 15,000 units with an estimated error of 1300 units. The forecast for the six months is 25,000 units. What is the measure of uncertainty in using this figure? This can be discovered by considering the extreme possibilities in the actual sales figure. If the two lowest possible sales figures occur for the quarters the final sales figure may be as low as 22,700 units (9000 + 13,700). If the two highest sales figures occur the final sales figure may be as high as 27,300 units. So that the final actual sales figure may lie anywhere between 22,700 units and 27,300 units. If for forecast purposes the sales figure is taken 25,000 units as suggested the error may be 2300 units in either direction. Thus is the sum of the two errors 1000 units and 1300 units.

When measurements are added the rule is that the error involved in the sum of the measurements is the sum of the errors in the separate measurements. Mathematically this can be shown as follows:

If the sum of the measurements a, b, c, . . ., etc., is denoted by S and if errors in a, b, c, . . . are denoted by e_1 e_2 e_3 . . . and the error is S by e then $S + e = a + e_1 + b + e_2 + c + e_3 + \cdots$ but $S = a + b + c + \cdots$
and therefore

$$e = e_1 + e_2 + e_3 + \ldots$$

The rule for discovering the degree of uncertainty in the product of two measurements is rather more complicated than in the case of addition and not quite so exact.

Suppose P is the product of two measurements a and b, so $P = ab$. Let e be the error in P and e_1 e_2 be the errors in a, b respectively.

Then
$$P + e = (a + e_1)(b + e_2)$$
$$= ab + e_1b + e_2a + e_1e_2$$
since
$$P = ab$$
$$e = e_1b + e_2a + e_1e_2$$

If the errors in the measurements are not very large then e_1e_2 will be very small relatively to $e_1b + e_2a$ and can be ignored. If the errors are very large this rule cannot be applied, but in that case the measurements are so uncertain that really no conclusion can be reached. Ignoring e_1e_2

$$e = e_1b + e_2a$$

with a bit of algebraic manipulation, this can be written

$$\frac{e_1 e_2}{e_1 e_2}(e_1 b + e_2 a)$$

or
$$e = e_1 e_2 \left[\frac{a}{e_1} + \frac{b}{e_2} \right]$$

The rule, therefore, is

Divide each of the measurements by their respective errors and add the results. Multiply this result by the product of the errors.

Consider the example of a long-term estimate of sales income. Income is the product of unit sales and price and if it is a long-term forecast there may be errors in both measurements. Suppose unit sales are forecast as 10,000 with an error of 1000 and price at £35 per unit with an error of £5. Sales income will vary between 9000 × 30 = £270,000 and 11,000 × 40 = £440,000 while the forecast of income is 10,000 × 35 = £350,000. The actual error in the forecast of sales income is £80,000 at the lowest limit and £90,000 at the upper limit. In the formula derived above

$$e = e_1 e_2 \left[\frac{a}{e_1} + \frac{b}{e_2} \right]$$

$$e_1 = 1000 \qquad a = 10,000$$

$$e_2 = 5 \qquad b = 35$$

Substituting these values in the formula

$$e = 1000 \times 5 \left[\frac{10,000}{1000} + \frac{35}{5} \right]$$

$$= 5000 \, [10 + 7] = 5000 \times 17 = 85,000$$

which is the average of the actual errors 80,000 and 90,000.

Uncertainty of Outcome

In addition to uncertainty in the measurements of the elements of a problem there is normally also uncertainty in the outcomes of possible decisions. If decision-making is to be realistic, some account must be taken of this type of uncertainty. The following is a typical example of such a problem.

The marketing director is about to decide which of two advertising campaigns put before him should be used. The first is keyed to a dry-weather concept and, it is considered, will be successful if there is not more than a given number of days of rain during the period of the campaign. The second is keyed to a wet weather concept and, it is considered, will be successful if there is more than that number of days of rain. The first advertising campaign will cost £20,000 and it is forecast that, if it is successful, sales will amount to £40,000 and if it is not successful to £8,000 only. The second advertising campaign will cost £12,000 and it is forecast that, if it is successful sales will amount to £35,000 and if it is unsuccessful to £8,000 only. What is uncertain is how many days of rain there will be.

If nothing at all can be said concerning the chances of rain the Pay-off Table shown in Table 38 tabulates the figures which will form the basis of the decision. Advertising Campaign One is denoted by A_1, and Advertising Campaign Two is denoted by A_2, while S_1 indicates that conditions are suitable for the success of A_1 and S_2 indicates that conditions are suitable for the success of A_2.

TABLE 38.
PAY-OFF TABLE

	S_1	S_2
A_1	+ £20,000	− £12,000
A_2	− £4,000	+ £23,000

The entries in each cell in a row are obtained by subtracting the cost of the appropriate advertising campaign from the sales forecast under each of the possible conditions in turn.

If no question of uncertainty arises the problem is trivial. If S_1 is certain, then A_1 is the right campaign to choose because + £20,000 is a better pay-off than − £4,000. If S_2 is certain, then A_2 is the right decision because + £23,000 is a better pay-off than − £12,000.

If there is a 50–50 chance of there being more than the required number of days of rain, so that the odds are evenly divided between S_1 and S_2, then intuitively no doubt the choice would fall on A_2.

The reasoning would run that with A_2 more would be gained if the choice is right than with A_1 and also, if the choice is wrong, less is lost with A_2 than with A_1.

Suppose, however, the scales are not evenly balanced, there being a 70% chance of S_1 coming up and only a 30% chance of S_2 coming up. What then? The consideration on which the choice is made is that if A_1 is chosen there is a 70% chance of £20,000 being gained and a 30% chance of £12,000 being lost, whereas if A_2 is chosen there is a 70% chance of £4000 being lost and a 30% chance of £23,000 being gained. It is still the case that, if the right circumstances arise, more will be gained if A_2 is chosen than if A_1 is chosen, but there is now much less chance that the right circumstances will arise. Similarly, if the wrong circumstances arise, it is still the case that less is lost by choosing A_2 than by choosing A_1, but there is now a much greater chance of the wrong circumstances arising. Stating the problem in this way provides a guide to the means of finding the solution. This is to identify for each of the possible solutions a measure of its value by taking into account the gain if the choice is right and the loss if the choice is wrong and the respective probabilities of being right or wrong.

This measure of value is found by multiplying the pay-off for each of the situations by the probability of that situation arising and adding the results algebraically, paying due attention to the sign of the pay-off. This measure is known as the *expected value* of the action to be taken.

Table 39 shows the result when this is done for the problem under consideration.

TABLE 39.
EXPECTED VALUE TABLE 70–30

Probability	S_1 70%	S_2 30%	Expected value
A_1	+£20,000	−£12,000	£10,400
A_2	− £4000	+£23,000	£4100

the details of the calculations being

$$A_1 = +0 \cdot 70 \times 20,000 - 0 \cdot 30 \times 12,000 = 10,400$$
$$A_2 = -0 \cdot 70 \times 4000 + 0 \cdot 30 \times 23,000 = 4100$$

With these probabilities A_1 is therefore the right choice to make.

Table 40 shows the expected values for a 50–50 split of probabilities.

TABLE 40.
EXPECTED VALUE TABLE 50–50

Probability	S_1 50%	S_2 50%	Expected value
A_1	+£20,000	−£12,00C	£4000
A_2	−£4000	+£23,000	£9500

The mathematical calculations confirm the intuitive judgement in this case that A_2 is the better choice.

A_2 is the choice for 50–50. A_1 is the choice for 70–30. At what level should the choice alter from A_2 to A_1? This will clearly be at the level where the expected value of A_2 is the same as the expected value of A_1. This can be calculated.

Let x denote the required percentage for S_1 so that the corresponding percentage for S_2 is $100 - x$. Hence $20,000x - 12,000 (100 - x) = -4000x + 23,000 (100 - x)$. When this equation is solved x is found to be $59 \cdot 3$ so that for all percentages for S_1 greater than $59 \cdot 3$ A_1 will be the right choice. The reader can check for himself that when the percentage for S_1 is 60% the expected values are

$$A_1 = £7200$$
$$A_2 = £6800$$

It is, of course, difficult in most cases to obtain reliable estimates of probability. It will be seen, however, that all that is required is to form a judgement as to whether the probability of one of the situations is above or below a certain level, in the example 60%. This is a very much easier task than to give a precise figure. When it can be done this is sufficient to identify the right course of action for every other probability even when the probability is not known with any certainty.

Supplementary Assessments

The probability estimates will in the main be subjective assessments based on the experience and judgement of those best qualified to know. However, the decision-maker may wish to avail himself of other opinions in order to support or cast doubts upon his own subjective probability estimates. Market test information might be commissioned or a second opinion sought. In the foregoing example the Meteorological Office might be approached for their estimate of the probabilities. Or if the figures are already those of the Meteorological Office then the advice of some unofficial local weather man might be sought in addition.

If the two opinions indicate the same course of action there will be no difficulty. Suppose, however, different actions are indicated. What then? The answer must lie in assessing the worth of the supplementary information and modifying the original opinion rationally in the light of this assessment. Two different assessments may be needed. One is the probability that if the second opinion confirms the first opinion both are right. The other is the probability that if the second opinion denies the first opinion the first opinion is nevertheless right and the second one wrong. Suppose in the example under consideration the probabilities of S_1 and S_2 are 70% and 30% as before but that now a second opinion is expressed that the probability of S_1 is less than 60%. Clearly there should be second thoughts. To what extent should the 70% figure be modified bearing in mind that different action will be taken if the probability of S_1 is reduced below 60%.

Bayesian Theory

A method of modifying probability estimates was developed in the early part of the 18th century by the Reverend Thomas Bayes, a Presbyterian minister who was also a mathematician. His theorem dealt with the probability associated with the occurrence of one event, given that another event has already occurred. This is known as *conditional probability*. If event B has already occurred then the conditional probability of A is denoted by $P(A/B)$ and is referred to as the probability of A given B. The concept may be extended to deal with several events.

Symbolically, several events are denoted by calling them A_1 A_2 A_3 ... and so on up to A_n, where n is the total number of events being considered. The probability of each of these events is denoted by $P(A_1)$ $P(A_2)$ $P(A_3)$ ... $P(A_n)$ respectively. If one particular event is to be considered on its own and it is not known in advance what the number of the event is, it is referred to as A_i and its probability as $P(A_i)$; i can, of course, be any number from 1 to n.

Bayes' Theorem provides a method of calculating a modified probability of an event whose probability has already been estimated from one source. It takes into account probabilities of the same event estimated from other sources and the estimates of the probability of two opinions which confirm each other both being right and also, where the two opinions contradict each other, of one or other event being correct nevertheless.

Suppose there are two events A_1 and A_2. In the example above they are the situations where the required number of days of rain do occur and where they do not. The probabilities of these are $P(A_1)$ and $P(A_2)$. $P(B_2/A_1)$ is the symbol for the probability of the second opinion contradicting the first opinion and the first opinion nevertheless being correct. $P(B_2/A_2)$ is the symbol for the probability of the second opinion confirming the first and both being right. Bayes gave a formula for calculating the modified probability which should be used as a basis for decision $P(A_1/B_2)$ in terms of these other probabilities $P(A_1)$ $P(A_2)$ $P(B_2/A_1)$ and $P(B_2/A_2)$. It is

$$P(A_1/B_2) = \frac{P(B_2/A_1)\,P(A_1)}{P(B_2/A_1)\,P(A_1) + P(B_2/A_2)\,P(A_2)}$$

In the example, $P(A_1) = 70\%$ and $P(A_2) = 30\%$. Suppose it is assessed that more reliance should be placed on this first opinion than on the second, if they differ, to the extent of being in the ratio of $4:1$, then $P(B_2/A_1) = 80\%$ and that $P(B_2/A_2)$ is assessed as 95%. This need not be 100% since it can still be granted that there is a chance of both being wrong. If both sources of opinion are considered very unreliable it may well be much less than 100%.

With these figures the calculation becomes:

$$P(A_1/B_2) = \frac{0\cdot8 \times 0\cdot7}{0\cdot8 \times 0\cdot7 + 0\cdot95 \times 0\cdot3}$$

$$= \frac{0\cdot56}{0\cdot56 + 0\cdot285}$$

$$= \frac{0\cdot56}{0\cdot845}$$

$$= 0\cdot66$$

That is the original estimate of the probability would be modified from 70% to 66% which would necessitate no change in the action to be taken since this modified probability is still above the 60% level where as was seen a change would be made in the decision. The implication of this result is that the first opinion is sufficiently strongly and reliably held as not to justify obtaining other estimates.

Suppose, however, the first opinion is not so strongly held and the assessment is that if a second source were to contradict it, one opinion could be reckoned as good as the other. In this case $P(B_2/A_1) = 0\cdot5$ and using the same formula $P(A_1/B_2) = 0\cdot55$.

Now the implication is different. It is that there is not sufficient confidence in the first opinion to withstand possible doubts cast upon it from another source. A decision based on it might easily be wrong and therefore a second opinion should be sought.

The general form of the formula when there are n events is

$$P(A_i/B) =$$

$$\frac{P(B/A_i)\,P(A_i)}{P(B/A_1)\,P(A_1) + P(B/A_2)\,P(A_2) + + + + P(B/A_n)\,P(A_n)}.$$

This formula is of particular use in considering how far subjective viewpoints should prevail and when on the other hand the time has come to look for second opinions either to support or refute the subjective view.

Applications of Bayesian Theory

Suppose, for example, discussion in the marketing department is centred round the possible introduction into the catalogue of a new product. The opinion of the marketing committee was that there was an 80 % chance of this new product doing well. However, the decision is postponed until the results of a market test are available. In deciding the details of the market test, it is laid down that if the sales in the market test do not exceed a certain level it is unlikely that the new product will sell well. The results of the market test show that the sales have not reached the level laid down. How far should the marketing committee adhere to their original opinion that the new product will therefore not be a good seller. This clearly depends on what is thought of the way the market test was carried out and the value of the results.

To apply Bayes' Formula it is necessary to make two assessments. These are:

(1) That if the market test shows poor results it will be wrong and the product will nevertheless be a good seller. Suppose this is assessed at 20 %.
(2) That if the market test shows poor results it will be right. Suppose this is assessed at 90 %.

Using these figures the modified marketing estimate of the new product being a good seller, calculated from Bayes' Formula is

48 % or roughly 50–50. The decision-maker is therefore faced with a marketing committee assessment that there is a 50–50 chance of the product being a success and a market test which indicates that it will not be a success. The decision must in the end depend on the view of the manager as to the level of certainty he requires to accept the marketing committee opinion in the teeth of contrary evidence.

Bayesian arguments can be used in conjunction with the calculation of expected values to give guidance on how worthwhile it is to seek additional information in situations of uncertainty. This can be discovered by applying Bayes' Theory and working out the expected values of the strategies available with and without information being available.

There are three stages of the analysis to which the names Prior Analysis, Posterior Analysis and Preposterior Analysis have been given. *Prior Analysis* consists of identifying the expected values of the strategies available in terms of the pay-offs of each and the probabilities allotted to each prior to obtaining information. This is the method previously explained.

Posterior Analysis consists of identifying the expected values in the same manner but with the prior probabilities modified using Bayesian Theory applied to extra sources of information available.

Preposterior Analysis takes the analysis a stage further by providing a comparison with the cost of obtaining the additional information.

Suppose the following values apply:

Expected Value after Market Test (Posterior Analysis)	£70,000
Expected Value before Market Test (Prior Analysis)	£55,000
Difference	£15,000
Cost of Market Test	£5000
Hypothetical Gain (Preposterior Analysis)	£10,000

Preposterior Analysis shows, therefore, that it is worthwhile paying anything up to something under £15,000 for a market test or other activity which will yield additional information. The criterion here has been assumed to be cash return, but conventional financial techniques can be incorporated in order to base the analysis on some other criterion.

The wider application of the theory requires much more sophisticated measurement techniques than have been introduced here but their exposition is beyond the scope of this book. Fundamental to them all are the theories of probability and an understanding of the elements of handling probability is essential for all who aspire to do marketing through measurement. This chapter, therefore, concludes with some basic rules concerning probability measurement.

Probability Measurement

The starting point is a scale of measurement. If there is no chance at all of an event occurring its probability is 0. Fixing the other end of the scale to give a value for absolute certainty is arbitrary. Conventionally, the upper value is fixed at 1. All probabilities are measured on the scale 0–1. The nearer the probability measurement is to 1 the more likely is the event to happen compared to an event whose probability measurement is nearer to 0.

Next it is defined that if two or more events are equally likely to occur then their probability measurements must be the same. So that if one or other of the events *must* happen the sum of the two probability measurements must be 1, and since they are equal each must be $\frac{1}{2}$. When a coin is tossed it must fall either heads or tails and the probability of getting a head is therefore $\frac{1}{2}$. So also is the probability of getting a tail $\frac{1}{2}$.

This can be extended to give a more general definition. If there are *a* equally likely events, one of which *must* occur, the probability of each is $1/a$. More general still, suppose that an event can happen in *a* ways and fail to happen in *b* ways, then the probability that the event will happen is

$$\frac{a}{a + b}.$$

As an example, suppose two coins are tossed together. What is the probability of getting two heads. The possible events are:

1st coin	2nd coin
Head	Tail
Head	Head
Tail	Head
Tail	Tail

There are four possibilities of which one produces the result wanted and three produce an unfavourable result. Hence the probability of getting two heads together in a tossing of two coins is $\frac{1}{4}$.

This method of measuring probability by considering all possible outcomes is known as *a priori* probability. However, knowledge of the causes of events may be very limited and experience of past happenings has to be called in to help. The definition is modified to declare that if in the past an event *has* happened, a fraction *p* of the total number of occasions on which it *might have* happened, then the probability of the event is defined as *p*. This is known as the *a posteriori* probability.

A posteriori probabilities can be used as the basis for future prediction so long as certain conditions are fulfilled. These are:

(1) That the sample of observations from which the probability was calculated was sufficiently large.
(2) That the sample was representative of all shades of opinion or occurrence relevant to the situation being investigated.
(3) That there will be no fundamental changes in the situation in the future compared with the past.
(4) That the selection of the events which have been measured has been done by a random process.

This requirement for randomness is the kernel of all applications of statistical probability. The validity of deductions from market research data such as were described in Chapter 2 depend upon it.

The probability of events occurring in combination has to be defined. Two main types of situation arise. Events may be mutually exclusive or they may be independent.

When events are *mutually exclusive* the situation is such that the occurrence of one event prevents tne occurrence of another. When throwing a dice one number only can turn up. It is not possible for any other number to come up simultaneously. Often, however, there is a need to know what is the probability of occurrence of one *or* other of mutually exclusive events. This is obtained by adding together the separate probabilities of the individual events. Thus in the dice example,

the chance of throwing a 2 is 1/6,
the chance of throwing a 3 is 1/6,
so the chance of throwing either a 2 or a 3 is $1/6 + 1/6 = \frac{1}{3}$.

The formal mathematical statement of the rule is that if the probability of occurrence of an event E_1 is P_1 and the probability of occurrence of another event E_2 is P_2 where E_1 and E_2 are mutually exclusive, then the probability of occurrence of either E_1 or E_2 is $P_1 + P_2$.

A special case of mutually exclusive events is the occurrence of an event and the non-occurrence of an event. These must be mutually exclusive and together they exhaust the possibilities. So if p is the probability of occurrence of an event and q is the probability of its non-occurrence, $p + q = 1$ and hence $q = 1 - p$. If the probability of occurrence of an event is known, the probability of its non-occurrence can always be calculated using this formula.

When the situation is such that the occurrence of one event does not affect the occurrence of another the events are said to be *independent*. Thus if a dice is thrown twice in succession the result of the first throw has no influence on the result of the second throw. The probability of occurrence of *both* of two independent events is the product of the separate probabilities of the individual events.

The probability of two heads coming up when two coins are tossed can be calculated using this rule since this is a case of independent events.

The probability of a head with one coin is $\frac{1}{2}$.

The probability of a head with the other coin is $\frac{1}{2}$.

So the probability of a head with both coins is $\frac{1}{2} \times \frac{1}{2} = \frac{1}{4}$.

This confirms the result obtained by *a priori* reasoning for this example earlier.

The formal mathematical statement of the rule is that if the probability of occurrence of an event E_1 is P_1 and the probability of occurrence of another event E_2 is P_2 where E_1 and E_2 independent then the probability of occurrence of both E_1 and E_2 is $P_1 \times P_2$.

Markov Chains

An application of probability theory to business forecasting occurs in the process of building what are known as *Markov Chains*. These are useful in forecasting the general state of business in situations of change. Suppose A denotes the state of business when business is good and B denotes the state of business when business is bad. Past experience shows that the chance of business remaining good for two successive weeks is 2/5 and that the chance of business remaining bad is $\frac{1}{2}$. These are *a posteriori* probabilities. Thus, in considering the state of business in two consecutive weeks, certain probabilities can be defined. These are the probability of state A in one week remaining state A in the next is 2/5; the probability of state A becoming state B in the next is 3/5; the probability of state B becoming state A in the next is $\frac{1}{2}$; the probability of state B becoming state B in the next is $\frac{1}{2}$.

These probabilities are shown in Table 41.

TABLE 41.
TABLE OF PROBABILITIES

| | | Next week | |
		A	B
This week	A	2/5	3/5
	B	$\frac{1}{2}$	$\frac{1}{2}$

The probability of a particular state of business at any time in the future can be built up using the table of probabilities and the rules for combining mutually exclusive events on the one hand and independent events on the other. Take, for example, the probability of business being good in three weeks time if it is good at the moment. The probability of each of a number of sequences must be worked out. These are:

	Now	Next week	Week 2	Week 3
1st sequence	Good	Good	Good	Good
2nd sequence	Good	Good ·	Bad	Good
3rd sequence	Good	Bad	Good	Good
4th sequence	Good	Bad	Bad	Good

If the required probability is denoted by $p(a)$,
$$p(a) = 2/5 \times 2/5 \times 2/5 + 2/5 \times 3/5 \times \tfrac{1}{2} + 3/5 \times \tfrac{1}{2} \times 2/5 + 3/5 \times \tfrac{1}{2} \times \tfrac{1}{2} = \frac{227}{500}.$$

The probability of business being bad $p(b)$ is accordingly:

$$1 - \frac{227}{500} = \frac{273}{500}$$

This can be checked by building $p(b)$ up:

$$p(b) = 2/5 \times 2/5 \times 3/5 + 2/5 \times 3/5 \times \tfrac{1}{2} + 3/5 \times \tfrac{1}{2} \times 3/5 + 3/5 \times \tfrac{1}{2} \times \tfrac{1}{2}.$$

These are examples are Market Chains.

These examples concern admittedly only very simple situations, but the principles remain the same for more complicated situations. For large models a computer may be an advantage in order to keep track of the complexities and to help with the calculation.

CHAPTER 8

FUTURE TRENDS

THE need for greater understanding of the marketing concept and for improvement in the effectiveness of the marketing function is constantly being stressed in many quarters. At the same time unfavourable comparison of the growth rate in the British economy with the rate in the U.S.A. is often accompanied by the comment that the explanation is to be found in the comparative effectiveness of the marketing function in the two countries. Be that as it may, there is no doubt that much fresh thought in marketing circles is currently being devoted to an analysis of the problems of marketing and to attempting to discern the main trends and changes affecting the role of the marketing decision-maker.

In the first place there is an increasing understanding that the relationships between a company and the environment on which it depends for its survival are now much more complex than they used to be. To expand this understanding greater use of existing techniques of measurement and the development of new ones is necessary. This expansion will be greatly helped by further development of equipment and expertise for data processing and information storage and retrieval.

Much of this development will be directed to determining future customer requirements. It would be naïve to suppose, however, that this will result in a complete understanding of all the significant variables in the marketing equation. The knowledge of customer requirements does not on its own form the basis of a research and development programme leading eventually to products tailored to those previously determined requirements.

Customers cannot necessarily determine their future requirements. If asked to do so they may attempt to co-operate, but there is no guarantee that when these hypothetical requirements can be satisfied the customer will in fact buy the products.

Professor J. K. Galbraith of Harvard has gone so far as to suggest that with the ever-growing capital investment of large corporations, it is almost unthinkable that success or failure of costly projects should be left to the whims of customer reaction. In *The New Industrial State* he postulates that "in addition to deciding what the consumer will want and will pay, the firm must take every possible step to see that what it decides to produce is wanted by the consumer at a remunerative price.

"So far from being controlled by the market, the firm to the best of its ability, has made the market subordinate to the goals of its planning. Prices, costs, production and resulting revenues are established not by the market but within broad limits . . . by the planning decisions of the firm."

There is not general acceptance that Professor Galbraith's words are a description of reality. Nevertheless, developed societies abound with examples of restriction of choice for customers through rationalisation of product lines and methods of distribution. The sentimental attraction of the little man, particularly in retailing, is rapidly being eroded by the cold economic facts of distribution, cost reduction and consequent lower prices in supermarkets and chain stores. Petrol companies are tending to rationalise their outlets following analysis of the cost of supplying low volume filling stations. Customers with comparatively bizarre requirements will have to pay to have them satisfied and the large corporation will embark on a substantial project only when it has satisfied itself that demand of a sufficient magnitude will be forthcoming for the resultant product or service.

If accepted, this means that the marketing decisions cannot be taken in isolation, concerning themselves with marketing factors only. The interaction between the marketing function and the other functions of a firm must be considered. Increasingly, therefore, the problems become more sophisticated and complicated and require more sophisticated techniques of thought-processing to unravel them. The trend will be towards a greater use of the techniques of operational research to provide the sophistication and more and more reliance will be placed on the electronic computer in order that the complication can be handled adequately within the time available.

Therein lies a danger. The belief must not gain ground that the possession of a computer and the representation of the problems requiring decisions in mathematical form are by themselves sufficient to guarantee that the right solutions will be reached. The electronic computer operates on data provided to it and "garbage in, garbage out" is both a well-known and significant remark concerning computers. Moreover, the mathematical expressions are the representations of the decision-maker's understanding of the problem. If his understanding is at fault then this detracts from the adequacy of the representation and the validity of conclusions drawn from it. To improve understanding of problems is an essential prerequisite of efficient decision-making and the marketing decision-makers of the last quarter of the the 20th century will be very much more knowledgeable about a great many more subjects than their predecessors.

There is a further danger that the manager may come to place so much reliance upon his computer that his inclination to think for himself dwindles away. Although, of course, it is true that small jobs as well as large can be fed into the computer, and although also it may be very handy to have all the jobs carried out by the computer, sometimes it may be at a cost which is not economically justifiable. For any problem there are as often as not several ways of discovering the solution. Consider the problem stated in Chapter 6 to be a Linear Programming problem. It was this.

The advertising manager is concerned with deciding how his advertising appropriation should be divided up. The conditions of the problem can be stated as follows.

(1) The choice of media are:
     television;

daily newspapers;
Sunday newspapers;
monthly magazines;
quarterly magazines;
and it is a matter of policy that all should be used.

(2) The maximum advertising appropriation that can be permitted is £500,000.

(3) For policy reasons the following spending limits are set:
at least £250,000 on television;
at least £50,000 on daily newspapers;
at least £1000 on each of the remainder.

(4) Exposures for each use are reliably estimated as follows:
300,000 for television;
200,000 for daily newspapers;
200,000 for Sunday newspapers;
50,000 for monthly magazines;
10,000 for quarterly magazines.

(5) The costs per use are known to be:
£15,000 for television;
10,000 for daily newspapers;
5000 for Sunday newspapers;
1000 for monthly magazines;
500 for quarterly magazines.

(6) Any number of uses in a year is permissible for each of the media up to the maximum possible.

Thus television should be given £250,000, daily newspapers should be given £50,000 and quarterly magazines should be given £1000. Since monthly magazines have the highest rating of attractiveness the maximum possible should be spent on that medium. Since there can be no more than twelve occasions on which the advertisement can appear in a monthly magazine, this is £12,000. The remainder must go to Sunday newspapers so long as this restricts the number of appearances in that medium to not more than 52, which it does. Thus Sunday newspapers should be given £187,000.

Table 42 shows these appropriations translated into number of appearances.

TABLE 42.

	Appropriation £	Number of appearances units (rounded down)
Television	250,000	16
Daily newspapers	50,000	5
Sunday newspapers	187,000	37
Monthly magazines	12,000	12
Quarterly magazines	1000	2

Using Linear Programming with or without a computer the same result would have been obtained. The technique achieves this by taking any possible solution as a starting point and by making successive trials of alternative solutions so as to improve the result until finally no further improvement is possible. What the common sense approach has done by contrast is to go straight to the final solution as a result of a judicious choice of measurement and decision rule. It still remains to prove that there is no better solution. In this example this is easy enough by comparatively simple logical reasoning. In more complicated examples it would be difficult to prove.

Contrary to the worst fears of many managers, hunch and judgement must continue to play their part in the decision-making process. It will, however, increasingly be the case that as more powerful techniques of deduction are developed and increasing use is made of the electronic computer, hunch and judgement will be removed from the actual process of reaching conclusions. Rather they will be applied at a very much earlier stage when the problem is being defined. Although the sciences of measurement can give much help, only the experience and intelligence of the manager can, in the last resort, fully understand the nature of his problems. The necessity for much earlier managerial intervention in the decision-making process is quite clearly seen when use is being made of a computer. Then, from information fed into it, the computer proceeds to make deductions and reach conclusions uninfluenced in its actual processing by managerial hunch, judgement and experience. This is understood and accepted by the manager in such a situation. Of course, he has freedom of action to reject the conclusion and to adopt any other decision he thinks fit. In doing so he may act as irrationally as he likes. If he wishes to act rationally there are really only two grounds on which he can do so and both reflect in some degree on his own efficiency.

One possible ground is that the technique is being applied inefficiently. If so the remedy lies in the manager's own hands and requires him to carry out his normal function of choosing staff wisely and maintaining adequate supervision. The other is that the information is erroneous or incomplete or both. If the correct information could have been provided in advance it is inefficient not to have done so. If the fact that the information is deficient has become apparent only after the processing had been carried out and it is not denied that the initial conclusions very often engender in the mind of the manager new thinking about his problem, the course is always open, if economically viable, to do the processing again, this time using the improved information. If the potential return from solving the problem is not sufficient to stand the cost of further computer runs, then it should be considered whether a hunch method of decision-making should not have been preferred in the first place or whether more time and money should not have been spent on information gathering and interpretation before the processing. Since it seems clear that greater use is bound to be made of the computer for data processing, the corollary seems equally clear that the manager as decision-maker must lay greater emphasis on his responsibility for defining the problem and less on the task of performing the reasoning process on the data.

This trend will be accentuated by a number of factors of which one of the most important is the continuing growth in the size of commercial organisations. The resources needed in modern technology in a wide and widening range of industries are such that only very large organisations can enter the ring. Supersonic aircraft, synthetic fibres, automobiles and many other products require very heavy investment in research and development, in production facilities and in marketing activities if they are to be commercially viable.

Both the rewards for successful and the penalties for unsuccessful decision-making are that much greater than they were. It becomes correspondingly more important to seek the *best* decisions in place of *good enough* decisions. The word best embodies a mathematical concept which the word good does not. It is not possible to discover the best of anything without comparison and it is not possible to have comparison without measurement. To disentangle meaning from measurements is a difficult business which the unaided human brain is not very good at. It needs help both from equipment and techniques and in taking advantage of that help it is moving away from hunch in the process.

Moreover, the changes in technology and economics are explosive. Experience of the past becomes less relevant to the future as changes in environment and practice become more rapid. Projection of past thinking to reach decisions which will apply in the future requires stable conditions if the decisions are to be adequate. When the conditions become unstable other forms of decision-making must be sought. This comes from the processes of deductive reasoning which are themselves stable. For this form of decision-making to be adequate requires a careful understanding of the nature of the problem. It is not a very worthwhile result to obtain the right answer to the wrong problem. The conclusions can be reached by formalised procedures. The specification of the problem, though science can help, is and seems certain to remain an area in which subjective judgement is still the all-important function.

Accompanying these developments of explosive growth is the increasing internationalising of business affairs. Not only is the market becoming international so that decisions have to be taken internationally, but communication systems are now so advanced that national barriers to the passage of information are eroded and data can be made universally and instantly available. What lags behind is the means of interpreting the information in such a way that all parties to a decision extract the same meaning from it. One of the obstacles is the fact that much of the measurement and interpretation is local and subjective in character. To overcome this obstacle the movement towards objectivity and standardisation must go on. This is not to deny that local and subjective influences play their part, but their significance in any particular situation will need to be assessed and they will have to take their appropriate place in the wider specification of the problem.

The development of effective techniques of measurement, coupled with progress in data collection and interpretation facilities, will inevitably materially affect management decision-making processes in the future. Many processes can indeed be completely delegated to machines. Numerically controlled machine tools, continuous process chemical plants and the automatic landing are only a few examples. In the field of marketing, computer controlled warehouses and automatic packing and scheduling of goods for delivery already occur. There will be many more similar examples as time goes on.

This does not mean that the manager will be superseded. As more and more functions lend themselves to numerate decision-making, more time will be available for those problems which do not. It will be one of the functions of the sophisticated information systems of the future to reduce the area of uncertainty in human affairs. It is never likely to be entirely eliminated and the reduced area where uncertainty remains will grow in complexity and require a deeper human understanding of its nature if decisions taken concerning it are to be satisfactory.

Moreover, every automatic operation requires initiation and a prepared programme of steps to be taken before it can operate. This again is a function of human thinking and although the horizon beyond automation can be pushed further and further back, it will always be there. In the area where man will still operate he can operate either by instinct or by logical reasoning. He may and will choose either. Instinct is the form of decision-making process practised by all orders of the animal kingdom. Man alone possesses a developed brain and man alone is capable of logical reasoning to any marked degree. The more he uses it and organises his means of measurement and interpretation of data the more certain is he to understand his problems and improve the quality of his decisions.

BIBLIOGRAPHY

ANSOFF, H. I. *Corporate Strategy*. Penguin Books 1968.
BATTERSBY, A. *Sales Forecasting*. Cassell, 1968.
GALBRAITH, J. K. *The New Industrial State*. Hamish Hamilton, 1967.
GREEN, P. E. and TULL, D. S. *Research for Marketing Decisions*. Prentice-Hall, 1966.
HUGO, I. ST. J. *Marketing and the Computer*. Pergamon Press, 1967.
JOHNSON, A. S. *Marketing and Financial Control*. Pergamon Press, 1967.
KEAY, F. *The Numerate Manager*. Allen and Unwin, 1969.
KOTLER, P. *Marketing Management*. Prentice-Hall, 1967.
LUCK, D. J., WALES, H. G. and TAYLOR, D. A. *Marketing Research* (2nd edition). Prentice-Hall, 1961.
MORONEY, M. J. *Facts from Figures*. (3rd edition). Penguin Books, 1956.
RODGER, L. W. *Marketing in a Competitive Economy*. Hutchinson, 1965.
SMALLBONE, D. W. *The Practice of Marketing*. Staples Press, 1965.
WILLS, G. *Marketing Through Research*. Pergamon Press, 1967.

INDEX